New Directions in Latino American Cultures

Series Editors
Licia Fiol-Matta
Department of Spanish and Portuguese
New York University
New York, NY, USA

José Quiroga
Emory University
Atlanta, GA, USA

The series will publish book-length studies, essay collections, and readers on sexualities and power, queer studies and class, feminisms and race, post-coloniality and nationalism, music, media, and literature. Traditional, transcultural, theoretically savvy, and politically sharp, this series will set the stage for new directions in the changing field. We will accept well-conceived, coherent book proposals, essay collections, and readers.

More information about this series at
https://link.springer.com/bookseries/14745

Arturo Chacón Castañón
Robert McKee Irwin

Listening to Sicarios

Narcoviolence in Ciudad Juárez, 2008–2012

Arturo Chacón Castañón
Departamento de Humanidades
Universidad Autónoma de
Ciudad Juárez
Ciudad Juárez, México

Robert McKee Irwin
Department of Spanish and
Portuguese
University of California, Davis
Davis, CA, USA

ISSN 1554-4028   ISSN 2634-520X (electronic)
New Directions in Latino American Cultures
ISBN 978-3-030-94117-8   ISBN 978-3-030-94118-5 (eBook)
https://doi.org/10.1007/978-3-030-94118-5

This Palgrave Macmillan imprint is published by the registered company Springer Nature
Switzerland AG.
The registered company address is: Gewerbestrasse 11, 6330 Cham, Switzerland

ACKNOWLEDGMENTS

Arturo Chacón is deeply grateful to his parents Soledad and Camilo and wishes to dedicate this book to Brenda and Oliver, his family, the fundamental pillar of his life and witnesses to his battles.

He is also thankful for the support of friends and colleagues who have accompanied him on this interesting voyage, among them FlorUrbina, Víctor Hernández, Eduardo Barrera, Salvador Salazar, Nicolas Valencia, Alex Pena, Alejandro Gómez, and especially his coauthor Robert McKee Irwin, for believing in his work.

He is also especially indebted to the individuals who bravely opened up to him and shared their experiences. This study would obviously have been impossible without them.

Robert Irwin thanks Flor Urbina of Universidad Autónoma de Ciudad Juárez for introducing him to Arturo, then a promising doctoral student, and to Arturo for trusting him to collaborate in this complex project.

We are both also appreciative of the support of Millie Davies, our editor at Palgrave Macmillan, and of Licia Fiol Matta and José Quiroga, the academic editors of the New Directions in Latino American Cultures book series, as well as the two anonymous peer reviewers who offered well-informed and unusually helpful insights on our manuscript. Our submission during the Covid-19 pandemic made the review process unusually difficult for everyone, and we are grateful to all those who believed in our project and helped to move it forward, even as we were all overwhelmed by the radically altered personal and professional circumstances and the day to day uncertainty the public health crisis generated.

CONTENTS

1   Introduction: Listening to Sicarios   1

2   Deadly Employment within the Border Industrial Complex   21

3   Youthful Murderers: Innocence and Professionalism   43

4   Sicario Masculinities: Feeling Reckless and Afraid   65

5   Fury as a Tool of Evil   89

Works Cited   115

Index   123

CHAPTER 1

Introduction: Listening to Sicarios

Arturo Chacón:

On the morning of January 31, 2010, a Sunday, my editor called me at six in the morning to alert me about a mass killing that had occurred in the south of the city, and to tell me to get there as soon as possible. I quickly dressed and set out, filled with dread, for a thirty minute drive. My first impression upon arriving in the neighborhood, Villas de Salvárcar, was unforgettable. From the moment I parked and got out of my car, I could see a large number of adults crying inconsolably, wandering about the street. The sun was just starting to rise. In that period of escalating violence, I had been witness to so many different scenes of crimes and violence, but I never managed to comprehend what had happened there.

I walked down the street searching for the address I'd been given, and soon saw a thick rivulet of blood that extended several meters from the entrance to a small and modest looking house. I had never seen so much human blood in the same place. Reaching the house required stepping across it, and I could feel its weight on the soles of my shoes. There was a small crowd of people, many weeping despairingly, out in front. I recall being overcome with the emotional intensity of the scene as I felt their eyes looking at me approach the house.

A heavily armed commando had broken into the house and opened fire on a party of teenage revelers. Most were shot dead at close range; only a few got away. There was blood all over all the bedrooms, and bullet holes everywhere. The building smelled of gunpowder, and was filthy with the viscous drying blood mixed with mud and pebbles that stuck to the soles of the shoes of everyone who entered.

© The Author(s), under exclusive license to Springer Nature Switzerland AG 2022
A. Chacón Castañón, R. M. Irwin, *Listening to Sicarios*, New Directions in Latino American Cultures,
https://doi.org/10.1007/978-3-030-94118-5_1

A man stood outside staring stupefied at the house without speaking. Journalists moved about trying to piece together the details of what had happened. I began speaking with the man, who told me he had been at home the night before watching television, when he suddenly heard a torrent of gunfire coming from the residence where his son was at a party. He found him on the floor; he didn't see any wounds and tried to lift him up. He was alive, but couldn't speak. He held his son's head up, but as he took his head in his hands he realized that he had been hit in the nape of the neck. He hugged his son to him as he gasped his final breaths. As he told his story, he broke down sobbing and kept repeating 'they took him away, "they took him away' [this and all subsequent translation from Spanish are ours] while rubbing his face with his hands, still stained with his son's blood.

Then I heard a girl who had been at the party telling people that several people had shown up in pickup trucks and quickly begun firing at everyone with 'cuernos de chivo' (AKA-47 assault rifles). 'Look at the bones,' she lamented. Only then did I realize that the pebbles that I had picked up on the bottom of my shoes were really small shreds of human bone, which had sprayed across the house.

I wondered upon meeting this ordinary looking father and hearing from this ordinary looking teenage girl what this implied about the extent of the bloodshed that was extending all over Juárez. This massacre seemed to mark a moment when everyone realized the violence had crossed a line; if in the past few years it seemed to be always dangerously nearby, but mainly confined to a certain class of young delinquents killing other young criminals of the same class, with the Villas de Salvárcar massacre, it entered brutally into the mainstream of Juárez society. Some early speculation assumed that some of the youth were themselves involved in the narcotics trade; however, this idea proved false. Investigations determined that in the wee hours of the morning, fifteen teens from the CBTIS-128 high school, mostly soccer players from the city's AA league, were mistaken by members of the Sinaloa cartel for members of a rival gang known as Artistas Asesinos, also AA. If high school soccer players could be easily confused with sicarios, i.e. if the sicarios couldn't tell the difference between narcos and teenage soccer players, how could Juárez find the dividing line between good and evil?

Listening to Sicarios

Much has been said about both drug related violence in general and the specific category of violence by hire, the professionalized serial acts of brutality on demand carried out by sicarios. There are studies focusing on the socioeconomic contexts from which sicarios are recruited with emphasis on such themes as lack of economic opportunities, the appeal of easy money, the projected glamor of gangster culture, psychological profiles and family histories of violent individuals, the extreme inequities of neoliberalist regimes, among many others (see e.g., Salazar, Ríos, Rivera González). Other studies seek to understand the broader structural components of violence, including those of unchecked globalized capitalism, persistent patriarchal ideologies, ever more rigid social hierarchies (see Reguillo, Reyna, Pérez Mendoza, Cisneros and Robles Rodríguez, Pérez Mendoza). Others focus on the histories and structures of drug trafficking as they relate to chains of production, mechanisms of distribution—at both wholesale and retail levels, including cross border smuggling, and consumption of narcotics across different social sectors, as well as the ways in which narcotrafficking interacts with law enforcement, judicial and legislative branches of government, and with other criminal and noncriminal enterprises (see Valdez Castellanos, Bataillon, Hurtado and García Paz).

The extremely antisocial behavior of individuals who seem in many ways to be quite ordinary has provoked a great deal of interest among scholars. Generally speaking, it is believed that most sicarios would never come to commit multiple homicides, perhaps not even a single significantly violent act, were it not for the circumstances that cultivated their emergence and proliferation. Unlike serial killers, sociopaths who would appear to be independent actors compelled by very particular psychological disorders that drive them commit destructive violence, or mass public shooters, who also are often loners whose atrocities are often motivated by hatred of social groups or institutions, or ideological obsessions, sicarios form integral parts of organizations that control and reward their actions, which have more to do with rivalries for economic and territorial control among different criminal syndicates than personal demons. They are in some ways more like members of military or paramilitary groups than mass or serial murderers, although their alliances with the organizations to which they belong are not based on conventional social contracts that morally justify violence through doctrines of national defense, or revolutionary ideologies in which participants may fervently believe, but rather on economic contracts, monetary compensation. The idea that ordinary people might be led to commit mass atrocities that are deeply damaging to the society in which they themselves, and their own loved ones, live, for financial gain, seems so radical as to be ethically inexplicable to many, who assume explanations must be found in the broader social contexts surrounding the violence.

A handful of books have focused attention on individual sicarios who have offered interviews, most notably *The Hollywood Kid: The Violent Life and Violent Death of an MS-13 Hitman* by Óscar and Juan José Martínez, and *El Sicario: The Autobiography of a Mexican Assassin* by Molly Molloy and Charles Bowden. Very few sicarios are willing to talk to outsiders; very few feel safe discussing acts that not only warrant severe criminal penalties, but also inspire broad public revilement. Likewise, the terrain of drug related violence is not one into which many academics, especially ethnographers, would dare to venture. No doubt, many researchers would shy away from entering into relationships with individuals who are known for their casual and callous treatment of human life, and for whom extreme forms of violence are part of day to day existence. Stories abound of journalists or even musical artists who had had frequent contact with drug syndicates and ended up murdered: the documentary filmmaker Christian Poveda, journalist Javier Valdez, and the popular narcocorrido artist Vicente Elizalde are a few of the best known. While the above mentioned texts offer rare glimpses of lives that are unimaginable, fascinating and shocking to many readers, and have consequently been best sellers, published testimonial narratives of sicarios remain few and far between. And the vast majority of those that have been published tell the story of a single assassin, whose personal idiosyncrasies may or may not apply widely across the trade—a notable exception being what is often cited as this genre's foundational text, *No nacimos pa'semilla* (published in English as *Born to Die in Medellín*), a collection of a half dozen testimonial narratives of young Medellín based sicarios recorded and compiled by Colombian Alonso Salazar in 1990.

In this landscape, where sicarios are understood as an increasingly critical social problem in need of solving, and in which an abundance of scholarship has weighed in with ideas, theories, and critical analyses, the absence of voices of sicarios is striking. A copious amount of scholarship addresses the issue, but mostly without turning to those best equipped to explain the phenomenon. Arturo Chacón, a journalist turned academic, who had been thrust into narcoviolence on his reporting beat, could not understand how the same kinds of kids he'd grown up with, had seen around town for years, were falling not into drug addiction or patterns of petty crime, but were suddenly becoming professional assassins. Although it was terrifying for him, he felt a need to hear directly from them, to listen to their explanations for how they ended up as sicarios, and what it felt like for them to follow this path. He sensed that they were both vile monsters and ordinary humans, but was perplexed at how to reconcile these two categories.

Arturo Chacón's field research, which incorporates material from interviews with a half dozen sicarios, is quite extraordinary. The archive he assembled, while not offering a statistically significant cross section of the demographic, does allow the coauthors to identify some patterns and tendencies. And although most of the interviews he managed to gather are not lengthy, there is sufficient material to draw some significant insights.

These insights are based on the assumption that the best source for explaining the choices and acts of sicarios is the sicarios themselves, and the best method of understanding them is to listen directly and closely to what they have to say. Sicarios themselves are the only ones who can speak from experience of their decisions to become killers, of the sensations they feel during and after an assassination, of the moral justifications or rationalizations they apply in electing to carry out violent acts, of their relationships to those who hire them, and of the decisions of some to leave the profession. We approach sicarios not so much as objects of study, but as knowledge producing subjects. We seek here not necessarily to endorse anything they may say as uncontestable facts, but rather to put their ideas and assessments into dialogue with the many theories and assumptions circulating about them, whether in academic or more popular venues. Without aligning specifically with any of the many decolonialist or subalternist approaches to testimonial narratives, much less fetichizing these narratives as somehow nobler, purer, or more accurate than other writings about narcoviolence, including those based on ethnographic, archival or journalistic research, we privilege in this book the voices of the sicarios themselves, not necessarily because we must attribute an inherent authority to them, nor because we can trust them to analyze and express the truth of their lives with any precision, but because among those who have sought to assess the phenomenon of the job category and career path of sicarios within drug trafficking organizations, they are the only ones with access to the thoughts, feelings and desires that have motivated their actions. Our aim here is to bring their own articulations of their lives to the table. We don't want to imagine the motivations and emotions of sicarios by relying a priori on theories or second hand knowledge regarding Mexican narcoculture, gang or cartel related violence, or contemporary youth from low income areas; instead we aim to listen first to what sicarios have to say, and then put their articulations and constructions of knowledge and experience in dialogue with the perspectives of academic theories and knowledge.

MEETING SICARIOS

The problem from the beginning, as indicated in the anecdote that opens this introduction, was to figure out how to meet sicarios and how to get them to speak in a way that puts neither these young men, nor their academic interlocutor at risk.

Chacón explains:

> *Throughout my training in the field of communication, and my professional trajectory as a journalist, I have always considered that those things that people can't easily verify or prove themselves are what most get their attention. Observing and documenting social phenomena, especially those that seem most impenetrable to outsiders, has been my habit since college. Ciudad Juárez has been seen as a social "laboratory" due to the duality determined by the intrinsic force of its thriving industrial labor market, and the lure of its geography at the extreme north of Mexico, just beyond the border of the United States, and there has been no better site than Juárez for understanding several different social and cultural phenomena of our times, ranging from the banal (the economics of the maquiladora industry) to the outrageous (feminicides and judicial impunity).*
>
> *What led me to undertake this project for my doctoral dissertation was the desire to understand, first, why it was that so many young men in our city were killing other young men; second, what led them to risk or destroy their own lives in doing so; and finally, to return to the scene of a crime, what I could learn from the killing of a childhood friend.*

The state's own deep participation in the exponential rise of deaths in a city that is not that large (at one point three million inhabitants as of 2010, it was Mexico's fifth largest) in a scenario that is not that of war, but rather of a more independently driven form of annihilation, has invited speculation on what was happening there, especially during the presidency of Felipe Calderón (2006–12). It seemed that Calderón's strategy for addressing narcoviolence, which he called a "war," was designed not so much to control, hinder, or eliminate drug trafficking, but rather to eradicate the lowest strata in the chain of command, a social cleansing at ground level and via horizontal means; without noteworthy arrests or seizures of contraband, at least in Juárez, the violence of the city's most violent years projected an air of simulation, except that the deaths of so many of its marginalized youth were very real. Although executions at that time seemed indiscriminate, the balance was tipped heavily toward young people living in poverty.

Chacón continues:

In December of 2009 a childhood friend, with whom I'd spent a lot of time back in the day, was murdered in a rapid burst of automatic gunfire. A group of men had entered his workplace to kidnap him, and when he put up resistance, they shot him dead. They hung his body outside the shop that he and his two brothers had inherited from their father. I arrived at the crime scene as a reporter, without any knowledge that I'd find my friend lying dead on the sidewalk. I can still remember the lost expression of his younger brother, who was sitting on the curb some five meters from the cadaver.

My friend was thirty years old. Unlike so many young men who were being killed, he had not grown up in abject poverty. Furthermore his dual citizenship afforded him benefits, options unavailable to many others. I couldn't make sense of what had happened. I couldn't believe that this could happen to someone I had known so well.

This homicide, like 98% of those in Juárez, was never solved.

At that time I was working for an organization known as Periódico Norte, and as a freelancer for international communications media such as CNN and The Washington Post, among many others that were becoming increasingly interested in covering the city's violence. Juárez had gone from 300 homicides in 2007 to 1600 in 2008, and that was only a prelude to the crisis of violence that this border city would experience over the next few years. Indeed for the next three it would be known as the most violent city in the world. International journalism turned its spotlight on that disastrous dusty city, which transitioned from bearing the stigma of too many dead women, which had been widely reported in global media since the mid 1990s, to that of dead men, without any attention to any economic or social gains achieved by its population over these years. Juárez was known simply as a graveyard, a killing field.

My work took me to scenarios that I knew nothing about, and I had to quickly figure out how to report on a "war," a conflict zone that journalists arrived every day from all around the world to cover, without realizing that this war was intangible. They constantly told me, "take me to the war, to the combat line," but there was never anything like that. The city was guarded by some 1500 soldiers and another 1500 federal police, who never managed to establish control. Public places of all kinds, all over the city, even those in areas with a heavy presence of security forces, were the scenarios of murders in cold

*blood. Journalists from Israel, Austria, Denmark and Germany couldn't con-
ceive whether this war in Mexico was formal bellicose combat or a more sponta-
neous armed conflict. My role in assisting so many international journalists
ended up being that of translating this very local violence in ways that would
make sense for consumers of global media. The role of sicarios drew my attention
not because of their importance as a new rank in the chain of command within
criminal groups, but rather because of the frequency their public acts came to
occupy the headlines, and everyday discourse.*

*As it became part of my everyday work to cover crime scenes and listen to
eyewitness accounts of victims, my own distress at discovering the impact on the
social dynamic of the city was unavoidable. I came to feel a special concern
about the effects of this sustained and systemized violence on the sectors most
directly exposed to its assaults, including not only the tragic demise of their
direct victims, but also haphazard dangers faced by bystanders, as well as the
secondary consequences for a new generation of war widows and orphans. I
wondered what had occurred in the lives of the sicarios who were committing
acts of such brutality (and thereby exposing themselves to the same brutality),
and how they learned to do it, and it occurred to me that only from them could
I get a glimpse into their worlds.*

*2008 saw the beginning of the most violent period in the history of Ciudad
Juárez. By November of that year there were nearly 1300 homicides, roughly
four per day. A few months earlier, in July, I had spoken with Armando
Rodríguez, known to friends as Choco, a locally renowned journalist specialized in security matters with El Diario de Juárez, the print journal with the
largest distribution and presence in the border region. His experience and reputation granted him access to sometimes privileged information, and I sensed
that some of his publications were putting him at risk. For example, he'd
reported on some armored trucks that authorities had seized, but later returned
to their owners; or a federal investigation that ended abruptly with the execution of the agents assigned to the case on the same day that they arrived in
Juárez. I asked him one day in the press room of the Juárez district attorney's
office whether he was afraid for his safety. He replied only, "no, not at all; if they
kill me now, there will be a big to-do for the district attorney." That year we
journalists bore witness to the daily rise in casualties to new levels that we didn't
believe possible, but were very real.*

*On November 13, 2008, I awoke and began my daily routine, getting ready
to get to work by 8: 00. I took a shower, and just as I was drying off I heard
eleven gunshots – I remember it well because I counted them. That was a time
when executions began to be carried out in public spaces, and it was becoming
common to hear bursts of gunfire all over the city. Just a few meters from my
house lived some city attorneys, and I immediately assumed that they had been
targeted. I remember telling my wife to go to work right away, before the traffic
backups around the crime scene made it too hard to get out.*

A minute later I got a call from Manuel Sáenz, the photographer who regularly accompanied me in the field, who asked me if I knew what had happened. He elaborated: "They killed Choco," and I realized right away that those were the shots I had heard. I got dressed quickly, noticed that my wife had already left, and as I went toward the door to leave, I felt an intense chill pass through my body. I felt a great fear about just opening the door. What if someone were waiting for me to come out to kill me, too? I stepped back and snuck a look out the window through the curtains. At that time there were rumors about the cartels starting to kill journalists; more specifically, I knew there they were using police radio frequencies to send out threats to journalists. Now I knew that these threats were not idle.

The cold blooded assassination of Choco was a watershed event for journalists in Juárez in that time. Armando was taking his daughters to elementary school when his killer approached his car and shot him in the chest. That day a lengthy parade of news reporters visited the crime scene as a gesture of support, and also of fear. In those last few months, I'd interacted frequently with Armando and we'd become close. That day I couldn't help remembering his words about the hypothetical case of an attack. The threats against him and the climate of violence outweighed the confidence he had felt. The loss of my friend and colleague, a fellow journalist, brought the overwhelming rise in violence home to me, and things would only grow worse over the coming years. The figure of the sicario's rise to prominence in Juárez in 2008 would not be an anomaly – it was here to stay.

FIELDWORK PROTOCOLS

The fieldwork for this project—based on face to face meetings with sicarios—implied significant methodological challenges. The interviews that Chacón was able to realize could not follow norms for sociological or anthropological ethnographic fieldwork. Beyond the basic ethics required in working with human subjects—ensuring that this research would not do any damage, nor or put anyone in danger, whether the sicarios themselves, their families, their colleagues, or their victims—he had be constantly ready to respond to unexpected developments, making frequent improvised adjustments in order to accommodate the particular preferences or demands of the sicarios who agreed to meet with him. With each meeting, he had to negotiate the kinds of sensitive issues or problematic events that each sicario might want to discuss, as well as the implications of these meetings and discussions for his own safety and that of his family.

An initial challenge was to identify and gain access to sicarios who would be willing to speak about their experiences with an academic. Personal relationships were key here—Chacón was able to turn to some friends and colleagues who happened to know people of the right profile, and who were trusted enough by these sicarios to feel comfortable asking them if they would be willing to meet with a PhD student from the Universidad Autónoma de Ciudad Juárez. These personal connections were the only way Chacón could conceive to establish relationships and gain the confidence of people with the appropriate background for the study.

From the outset, his research aimed to understand sicarios from a human perspective, beyond the sensationalized, romanticized, and vilified images that appear on the news, in corridos, in telenovelas, and in social media. It was to be a scientific study that sought to get at the truths of lived experience. He wanted to understand the everyday aspects of the work life and culture of sicarios in Ciudad Juárez, with a focus on their motivations, thoughts, sentiments, reactions, and concerns regarding their work.

Safety was a key word throughout the study. The entire data gathering process was unpredictable. Opportunities could arise at any time, and when they did, they would require an immediate reaction. And despite precautions, Chacón was never fully in control of any situation, and any meeting with a new sicario presented new risks. He needed to commit to maintaining anonymity and not name names (to be clear: all names used to refer to interviewees in this study are pseudonyms), to describing events in ways that would never allow anyone involved, including victims, to be identified. From there he would set up a protocol tailored to any preferences articulated by the individual interviewee that would minimize risks to both of us. The interviews were limited to free sicarios—that is, those who were not currently incarcerated, although he did have the occasion to meet with on 16-year-old, who was being held in a juvenile detention center at the time of the interview. All had withdrawn from the criminal groups that had once employed them as assassins. Nonetheless, he had to be careful in cultivating relationships with these young people, maintaining a neutral tone no matter how emotional or shocking the stories they told. He had to be very sure to be respectful, free of any prejudices, and never judgmental. Basically, although it was not easy, he had to avoid viewing them as cold blooded killers, to see them instead as people, and to empathize with them, while maintaining a professional distance, making clear at all times that he would always be a researcher interested in their stories, but would not become a friend.

It was not possible to apply a specific or detailed questionnaire or a rigid plan for interviews. These subjects usually preferred brief meetings, and in some cases, it was not possible to meet more than once. These were never relaxed and low key interviews held in public cafés. Instead, they had to take place in private enough places that no one could eavesdrop, such as in a car driving around, in a park, in a safe house or an interviewee's apartment, or at a church. In addition, all of the interviewees had their own agendas and set their own limits. Some were eager to speak about certain themes, while utterly unwilling to address others. It was therefore essential to let the sicarios take the lead in deciding what to reveal, and to find opportunities to insert key questions—questions that would not provoke resentment or mistrust—when Chacón's intuition indicated an opening that would not cause discomfort. Their motives for agreeing to speak to him, and for trusting him, were quite diverse. For these reasons, each meeting was different—varying often significantly in length, content, and degree of detail, and it is not possible to generalize findings from them. Each interview ended up focusing on certain stories or anecdotes, and some provided more insights than others. But all offer interesting qualitative data.

While Chacón at first thought of them as radically alien, and had to be very careful in his performance of neutrality and empathy, after just a few interviews, he came to realize that these were in many ways very ordinary people, from ordinary families, whose fears, tastes, and aspirations were also quite ordinary. Their humanity was apparent even in the telling of the most brutal acts. And he was thus drawn in, probing ever more deeply into the uncertainty of what lie beyond the statistics, to understand those homes that have lost a member, those young people who didn't live to tell their stories—and who indeed may have had the same kinds of ordinary backgrounds, sentiments and motivations as those he was interviewing.

On one occasion in 2017, one of these young men agreed to speak to him at the former sicario's own residence. His story was like that of many others in terms of his recruitment, his beginnings, and his development as a sicario—but not in the story's ending. His jail time and the death of his brother led him to take a spiritual path that to this day has kept him alive and safe. Chacón interviewed him twice at his home, in his living room, in an extraordinarily impoverished living space, with his young children looking on, attentive to the presence of an outsider in the house. In his measured voice, he recounted, as if telling a story appropriate for any audience, the details of his process of becoming a sicario. Regretful, he explained that the hardest thing for him was facing having put his family at risk, and he stressed that leaving his former life as a sicario had not been easy—but that it was also not impossible. He was 39 years old but looked 50; he had lived through a lot, but he was convinced that religion had saved him from certain death. Now he had a steady job, earning a fifth of what he had as a sicario. He no longer had a car, weapons, luxuries; he was just getting by, but had managed to find a way to establish a new life that did not put his family's lives at risk. After telling his entire story, he told Chacón that he had wanted to share it in order to help others, so that others might avoid experiencing everything he had. He explained this while embracing his teenage daughter, and with his small son sitting nearby in the living room, observing.

Some reactions surprised Chacón, including those of informants who expressed feelings of lack of self-worth, saying they didn't deserve anything in life after what they'd done. They'd earned money, which allowed them to support their families, but otherwise were on a downward spiral, alienated from society, always on the run, falling ever backward in a state of agony. The opportunity to speak to some of them allowed Chacón to understand, if not fully comprehend, the gap between their parallel lives as ordinary young men, and deadly sociopaths, two sides that as much as they themselves might try, they were never able to convincingly reconcile.

Carrying out research under these circumstances meant stirring up deep feelings, evoking situations that Chacón had witnessed, whether as a news reporter or a resident of Ciudad Juárez during its most violent years. Sometimes it was very difficult for him to return home, where he couldn't speak about or share details of these meetings with his family—or even articulate the emotions he was feeling. Just as the lives of sicarios were not simple, it was not a simple task to listen to their telling, or to try and understand them. It was not possible to avoid strong emotional reactions upon hearing their stories, and there were times when uncertainty about the value of his research overshadowed any feelings of accomplishment evoked by what he was learning. Luckily he was able to count on colleagues, friends, and family, who gave him the strength to see through on this difficult fieldwork, in hopes that this book might add, albeit modestly, to the understanding of the roads taken by these young people that has made such an impact on the lives of those around them.

COLLABORATIVE ANALYSIS

The unique contribution of this study is its focus on first person narratives of sicarios. Our archive makes possible this communication from one of the most feared, abhorred, and poorly understood sectors of contemporary society to the world. The archive is indeed unusual because of how difficult it was to obtain. This difficulty makes it irregular, fragmentary. Interviews tended to be brief and topics of discussion were limited to what the sicarios were willing to share. Although anonymity was a premise for all discussions, fear of exposure, whether to law enforcement, rival groups, current or former colleagues, or one's own family, placed limits on every exchange. Arturo Chacón alone conceived of, planned, and eventually—in short bursts on those occasions when willing subjects materialized—carried out the fieldwork of this study, and is the lead investigator of this collaboration.

Robert Irwin joined in only later, when nearly all of the fieldwork was complete. Chacón initially asked him for help in translating this research, already published as part of his doctoral dissertation, into an academic study for the US market. Quickly a series of conversations between the two led to a decision to reshape the project together, setting the stage for what became a much deeper collaboration. Irwin had recently served as an expert witness in a trial of a Mexican immigrant accused of murdering another immigrant whom he'd met on the job pruning and harvesting grapes in Napa, California. As author of a book called *Mexican Masculinities*, which explored complicated intersections between Mexican ideologies of national manhood and male sexuality (including homosexuality) among Mexican men, he was asked to evaluate a series of sexually suggestive text messages exchanged between the victim and the alleged murderer, who prosecutors claimed had killed his colleague in order to erase a debt that he didn't want to pay.

Given Irwin's background, a PhD is in comparative literature, prior fieldwork consisting of many long hours in archives, and methods of analysis largely comprised of close readings of cultural texts, he had never considered that he might spend an afternoon in the Napa County jail interviewing an accused murderer. He realized that afternoon that the extreme context of homicidal violence among men struck a nerve, inspiring an unusual curiosity that led him to drive that afternoon around Napa visiting several key sites of interactions between these two men. Napa, known for its striking landscapes of grape orchards, seems idyllic in comparison to the mean streets of Juárez, another world. Yet, Irwin wondered after his initial discussion with Chacón, maybe there were cultural connections. The case, based on circumstantial evidence, ended in acquittal, with testimony from a different witness pointing to a second suspect, and introducing evidence that the killing may have had to do with a dispute regarding the sale of marijuana that the victim apparently grew and sold to local distributors, members of a criminal gang.

In addition to the intriguing subject matter, Irwin was attracted to Chacón's methodology. He had recently launched a digital storytelling project in Tijuana focused on deportation that also took a grass roots approach, looking to "migrant knowledge," and committing to listening to migrant stories in order to better understand the human consequences of contemporary migration control regimes (see Irwin and Alonso). In facilitating the production of the digital stories of several dozen migrants in Tijuana, Irwin came to appreciate both the eloquence of migrants in recounting their experiences, and the embodied knowledge they would often impart through their testimonial narratives. He was curious to hear the stories of the sicarios, and curious as to what wisdom they might offer.

This approach of listening emerges from decolonial theories, although its context is not one whose relationship with the coloniality of power can be laid out in simple terms (Coronil). If the social position from which sicarios tend to emerge is the product of the coloniality of power, their own approaches to and interpretations of their aspirations, decisions, actions, thoughts, and feelings do not necessarily challenge the kinds of social hierarchies that decolonial theory contests. Nonetheless, we find the decolonialist concept of border gnosis useful in analyzing the narratives of sicarios, as their world is one that seems separated in fairly absolute terms from those of the mainstream of Mexican or North American society. To be clear, border gnosis, as introduced by decolonialist scholar Walter Mignolo refers to a kind of "subaltern knowledge" that takes form at the margins, at the frontiers, of the modern world (*Local Histories* 13). It is difficult for those of us who have never crossed into the realm of drug cartels to have a clear idea of what it is like to live and work within them, especially in their most violent enclaves. For many it may be easier to understand the motives of behavior of individuals living on the other side of the world, who speak languages we've never heard spoken, whose religions are mysterious to us, and whose traditions are opaque to outsiders, but to whom we might imagine sharing some universal values or fundamental ethics. Sicarios, in this scenario, are assumed to be utterly different from us in some intrinsic way: they are prone to commit, on a daily basis, acts that are unthinkable to many. Some have gone so far as to define them as not entirely human, but perhaps of a different species, monstrous beings, "endriagos" (Valencia).

In this sense those of us who have not been sicarios or lived closely among them may not be capable of understanding them in a way that does not exoticize them—just as we might be likely to exoticize microcommunities of indigenous people living in remote locales by being able to conceive of their lives only through our occidental gaze. However, members of those communities who are also familiar with mainstream life in North America may be sufficiently circumspect and thoughtful to engage effectively in what Walter Mignolo has called "border thinking"—thinking across epistemological systems, or what he refers to as "that of the murmurs of modernity's dispossessed" ("Un paradigma otro" 133). Sicarios, who were born and educated in the mainstream of North American society, have no deep background differences from their neighbors, who may be employed in more legitimate, legal occupations. However, they have departed from societal norms in assuming the job of paid assassin, crossing a line from widely shared notions of humanity into the shadowy realm of monstrosity. Much as we may have access to studies regarding the backgrounds from which they emerge, the world into which they enter as sicarios remains unknown, nearly impenetrable to all except those who have lived there, or otherwise spent time directly observing its day to day workings. Most of us are unwilling to pursue either of these options, imagining it only through bits of information filtered through news media or fictionalized in movies, corridos, telenovelas, or other genres of cultural production. However, the fact that a handful of sicarios have offered to discuss their lives, translate their motivations and sentiments for an audience on the other side, that of a mainstream human North American world, gives us a unique glimpse into this sicario underworld. Indeed, the sample of testimonial narratives that form the archive for this study indicates that sicarios, whose observations are often surprisingly circumspect, and quite astute, can be effective border thinkers.

Regarding the articulations of sicarios that we analyze here, we have no illusions regarding our access to unmediated truth. Clearly both the notion of "mainstream" and "sicario underground" are imagined, constructed concepts, and there is no reason to assume that a random sicario is likely to be a deep border thinker, capable of thoughtfully translating his actions and feelings fully and accurately for a broad audience. Nor is there any reason to believe that any individual sicario's reconstruction of his acts, thoughts or feelings will be representative of anything generalizable or significant for coming to an understanding the collectivity of sicarios, even within the local context of Ciudad Juárez during the specific period at hand. Furthermore, we cannot make the argument that sicario testimonial narratives are unmediated by any range of popular images of sicario lives and lifestyles that may shape their own performances in those roles, as well as their recollections of or reflections on those performances. However, there is no doubt that sicarios, who have a different kind of access to the world on the other side of the imagined border between mainstream and narcosphere, are worth listening to. And we did listen to them; even when some of the stories turn especially violent or tragic, they are often quite gripping. It is hard not to pay attention.

Once we did listen carefully to them, several questions began to take shape. While their stories confirmed some ideas that have been well developed in scholarly or even in popular discourse, there were a few themes that presented some surprises, complications, nuances, contradictions that we thought to be worthy of our own reflection. Thus, we chose to orient our close readings of the sicario interviews from a handful of different angles, with each of us approaching this archive from our own areas of expertise, Irwin focusing on questions of border and gender, Chacón on youth and violence, as well as the historical and cultural context of Ciudad Juárez, where he has lived all his life, worked extensively as a journalist, and carried out his PhD research. While each took on the elaboration of certain sections of the manuscript, the writing process was dynamically interactive. If Chacón was the originator of the project, having carried out all the ethnographic research himself, Irwin finished it out, translating Chacón's Spanish language chapter drafts into English. In the end, while Chacón without any doubt deserves credit as this book's first author, the production of this manuscript was deeply dialogic and collaborative.

Themes and Insights

After extensive review of the narratives, we elected to focus in on four themes, which can be expressed through the key words border, youth, masculinity, and evil, and which gave shape to the following four chapters, each summarized below.

The first chapter, which closely follows the stories of two different sicarios, clarifies several ways in which growing up in the US Mexico borderlands might be especially conducive to personal trajectories that culminate in deep and perhaps violent involvement in the drug trade. The stories of these two young men track the gradual intensification of their criminal acts from petty smuggling to murder, as well as their roles as laborers, in fact as salaried assassins, within the ranks of drug trafficking organizations. Eschewing formal higher education, they learned their trades on the street or in prison, within the intensified criminal context of borderlands smuggling and trafficking. Their stories make clear that just as much as the maquiladoras where they might have ended up had they not chosen lives of crime, the drug trafficking business is best understood not as a separate underworld, but rather as a significant and integral component of the US Mexico border industrial complex.

The second chapter seeks to tease out what it means for minors to commit heinous crimes for which some believe they cannot be held fully responsible due to their immaturity. Those too young to vote, to engage in consensual sexual relations, to drink or smoke, to serve in the armed forces, would seem to be too young to assume full blame for committing acts of extreme violence and loss of human life. We look to the testimonial narratives of several different young sicarios to try to ascertain how they understand the divide between youth and adulthood by interrogating specifically how they describe transitions into the sicario trade—the points at which young sicarios become fully professionalized and conscious of the moral weight of their actions, and also at the ways in which sicarios differentiate between potential victims as being children (innocent victims) or adults (legitimate targets), not based on their age but rather on their actions and their implicit awareness of their responsibility for those actions. There is a nearly imperceptible line between innocent and foolish youth and fierce adulthood that sicarios seem able to instinctively sense, and feel compelled to try to explain.

The question of masculinity, explored in this book's third chapter, also arises in complicated and sometimes paradoxical ways in sicario narratives. Here we analyze the constructs of masculinity that surround and inform the lives of sicarios, including traditional notions of Mexican machismo, and its contemporary extreme variant, the masculinity exercised by the monstrous figure of the endriago. The chapter looks at both the aspects of orthodox notions of masculinity, most especially within the context of

Mexican culture, that characterize the self-representations of sicarios, along with several contrasting traits and tendencies that emerge repeatedly in their narratives that seem to radically contradict these norms. This chapter focuses in on the sicarios' expressions of sentiment, the kind of emotional responses they most emphasize in the telling of their stories, signaling the difficulties in achieving and maintaining manifestations of hypermasculine strength and pride without falling simultaneously into feminized expressions of fear and regret.

The final chapter turns to a fundamental question underlying the massive violence produced in the context of Mexican narcotrafficking, that of good and evil. This final reflection focuses on a single sicario narrative in order to try to make sense of two vastly different understandings of sicario agency. One assumes drug violence to be a destructive force motivated by greed and exercised with an utterly inhuman lack of concern for human life, and a monstrous arrogance in the face of the terror and havoc it wreaks: sicarios are sociopaths who need to be stopped, punished, and even annihilated. The other looks to identify underlying socioeconomic circumstances that may lead good people, especially young and impressionable ones whose life circumstances leave them highly vulnerable, to do bad things. This latter approach eludes assigning moral responsibility for violence to those who commit it, but instead identifies institutional factors, including state corruption, media sensationalism, inequitable access to education, economic exclusions wrought by global neoliberal capitalism, class and racial hierarchies, to name a few, that collectively may be to blame for the kinds of violence produced within drug trafficking organizations. Sicario narratives conform to neither of these ideas. Sicarios recognize some of the same social problems mentioned above, but refuse to see themselves as victims of unfortunate circumstances. Instead, they portray themselves as social actors who make decisions that lead them to commit acts that may be horrible or evil; but they both insist on their own agency, and on their humanity. They see themselves as committing evil acts—sometimes justifying them through particular idiosyncratic interpretations of good and evil—while retaining an innate humanity that in many cases leaves open the possibility for them, should they survive, to leave behind this period of their lives, and return to a life of nonviolence. Their labor as sicarios marks them for life, but does not define who they are at their core—a conclusion that they struggle to reach and to sustain, but is essential to their reintegration into society.

A Few Final Words

We believe that our observations in each chapter, and the testimonial evidence on which they are based, offer helpful interventions into contemporary scholarly debates on the themes at hand, and taken together make a modest contribution to understanding the violence that became so shockingly prominent, so gruesomely destructive, and so distressingly uncontainable in Ciudad Juárez in the first decade of the new millennium—and has emerged in different sites in Mexico, including once again Juárez, off and on since then. To be clear, our intervention here is not meant to correct existing theories or academic consensus regarding the lives, acts, motivations, or emotions of sicarios, but rather to offer new insights that might enrich discussions on these topics. We don't propose that this archive, taking into honest account its limitations, should be seen as definitive; however, since it offers some modest breadth of difficult to obtain direct, first person evidence, and assumes the aura of authority of lived experience, in sharp contrast with the mostly more anecdotal or otherwise distanced materials on which much existing research and theorization on these issues is based, we believe it to be highly significant.

CHAPTER 2

Deadly Employment within the Border Industrial Complex

This chapter argues that several broadly understood assumptions regarding sicarios are not necessarily true. Firstly, the paid assassins interviewed for this study do not identify as sicarios—it is not a term they attach to their identity. Rather, these young men view their experience killing as temporary, a job they took on for a period. Furthermore, none describes feeling coerced or even forced by circumstances into this professional line of work; they realize they had other options, but were attracted by the easy money, the prestige, the feelings of power. Nor have they felt obligated to remain in this job forever—until they are killed, or are given a life sentence (or death sentence). Instead, they describe a series of borderlands dynamics in which they pursue job opportunities in crime that lead them into employment by drug trafficking syndicates, in which they eventually end up working for a period of time as paid assassins. They are not innate murderers, nor are they obligated by desperate circumstances, nor are they compelled to act against their will, nor are they left with no way to escape. It might be helpful to think of the demand for slaughter as a function of the contemporary Border Industrial Complex, that is, the assemblage of interrelated structures and mechanisms designed to control the movement of people and products across the international border between the United States, and others designed to circumvent those controls. Sicarios—along with border patrol agents, maquiladora workers, coyotes, drug smugglers, call center agents, sex workers, health tourism entrepreneurs—are just one

A. Chacón Castañón, R. M. Irwin, *Listening to Sicarios*, New Directions in Latino American Cultures, https://doi.org/10.1007/978-3-030-94118-5_2

more borderlands job lines. Those who become sicarios might at other times of their lives hold other jobs; their experience in murder no doubt makes a huge impact on their lives and their psyches, but it does not necessarily define them.

THE BORDER CRIMINAL INDUSTRIAL COMPLEX

I started out at first stealing cars, that's right, stealing them in the United States and bringing them back over here, or stealing cars here, stereos, all of that; then I began getting involved, yeah, in packing bricks of marijuana, we began to pack, to pack, to load up cars to cross over there [...] (Salmo)

Salmo's induction into the illicit narcotics business began with cross-border smuggling. His rise up the ranks from car thief to sicario involved crossing the border dozens of times. In his study of the integral role of smuggling in the history of the United States, Peter Andreas argues, "we have always imposed restrictions on cross-border economic flows, and these restrictions have created all sorts of incentives and opportunities for smuggling" (6). It might be said that the fortification and securitization of the historically porous and US Mexico border over the past few decades has invited the Mexico based drug trafficking business to establish an increasingly intense presence and dynamic activity along Mexico's northern border. Just as young people growing up in economically depressed border areas of the southwestern United States might get recruited to become border patrol agents (Miller 57–82), young Mexicans like Salmo might be enticed to seek their fortune with drug cartels. We argue that both institutions form part of what Michael Dear has called the Border Industrial Complex.

While Dear defines the Border Industrial Complex as a US state apparatus of border policing that operates radically apart from, even in opposition to, the criminal activities of Mexican drug cartels (145–46), in our view both are industries whose primary activities are fostered by the border itself and ought to be thought of as part of a large transnational Border Industrial Complex. Dear's opposition between government sanctioned law enforcement agencies and illicit organizations, both of which exert their own forms of violence on marginalized populations in the borderlands, generating exorbitant profits for commercial enterprises that exploit the vulnerabilities of targeted groups (undocumented migrants, drug addicts, impoverished youth), seems artificial and arbitrary. Sandro

Mezzadra and Brett Neilson propose a method for the study of contemporary borders worldwide that emerges from a distrust in such dichotomies; their approach to borderscapes, of which a highly prominent and intense one is without a doubt that located on and around the US Mexico border, is "relational," one that addresses "the experiences of border crossing and border enforcement" while remaining deeply attentive "to the equivocations of definition, space, and function that mark the concept of the border itself" (10). Sergio González Rodríguez has argued provocatively that "the CIA [...] maintains links with criminal organizations in order to foster destabilization in Mexico" (23) as part of a larger plan to pursue "the absorption of Mexico's natural, energy and human resources in order to strengthen [the US's] geopolitical interests in exchange for financing, advising and surveillance" (26). Without necessarily endorsing either of these positions, ours assumes a similar stance that is deeply suspicious of binary oppositions, and assumes that the study of the borderlands must begin with attention to nuance. In this vein, a critical analysis of the US Mexico border requires thinking through the infrastructures of border security and those that interact with them—those that are affected by them and that provoke different reactions from them—as an assemblage of interdependency.

While it seems almost a cliché to quote Gloria Anzaldúa's brilliant 1987 essay/manifesto *Borderlands, La Frontera: The New Mestiza*, the rise of the Border Industrial Complex over the past three decades makes many of its author's observations all the more timely 30 odd years later. Anzaldúa writes, "The US-Mexican border *es una herida abierta* where the third world grates against the first and bleeds" (25). The securitization of the border from the US side has made the cross border smuggling business, whether of humans or of merchandise, most especially drugs, not only more necessary and more profitable, but also substantially more violent, and various powerful institutional protagonists within the Border Industrial Complex on both sides of the border are together responsible for the damage they cause. As González Rodríguez has argued regarding the past few decades, "Borders, strategic zones of tension, became porous, ductile, fluid," feeding both "the military machine and the criminal machine" (96). Likewise, many experts argue that Mexican state led efforts of securitization, including most notably its "war on drugs," waged with a spectacularized visibility in border cities known to be strategic points of narcotics smuggling such as Ciudad Juárez and Tijuana, contributed directly to the rise of drug cartel related violence, most especially during the presidency of Felipe Calderón beginning with his 2007 declaration of a "war on drugs" (see, e.g., Boyce, Banister and Slack).

To be clear, the scenario, in our view, is not one of US Homeland Security agencies (and all of the commercial interests that they serve—those that construct border walls, develop sensor technologies, run for profit immigrant detention centers, etc.) pitted against Mexican criminal networks. Rather, in order to understand the dynamics of border violence (or any other phenomenon occurring in the context of the US Mexico borderscape), it makes more sense to think of the transnational conjuncture of assemblages that include both sites of conflict, but also those of alliance, in this case between US and Mexican government agencies—evident, for example, in the Mérida Initiative, a security oriented agreement of cooperation between the United States, Mexico and the seven nations of Central America, aimed at controlling narcotics trade, that went into effect in 2007—or between drug traffickers and corrupted government officials or transnational state sponsored infiltrators.

At the borders between nations, and also between criminal syndicates and the government institutions meant to control them, leakages abound. Sonja Wolf's assessment of the Mérida Initiative is instructive. Wolf scrutinizes both the diplomatic agreement itself and its antecedents, going back to the 1980s and 1990s, with its signing in 2007 by presidents George W. Bush and Felipe Calderón, the latter noting at the time that Mexican drug cartels had significantly penetrated Mexican state institutions. She argues that Calderón's eagerness to launch the agreement was a political gesture meant to demonstrate his commitment to combatting drug trafficking and to legitimate his contested election to the presidency, but that the this initiative promised little to address the root problems of drug smuggling across the US southern border, amidst the an unfaltering demand in the United States, and the largely unaddressed corruption in Mexico that make it difficult to significantly curtail wealthy criminal organizations. Fourteen years later, her arguments stand. What has changed most over that period is the investment in border security and militarization, and a no doubt parallel investment in smuggling technologies, money laundering, and manipulation of high powered government players. The latter most recently played out in the arrest of Salvador Cienfuegos, former Mexican defense minister, who was detained in the US on multiple drug and money laundering charges, but soon thereafter returned to Mexico under pressure from the Mexican government, where he was investigated, and officially cleared of all charges. All of the above has translated to substantial growth of the Border Industrial Complex.

Furthermore, the fragmented networks of narcotics trafficking make it difficult to think of the crossborder drug trade as a single unified force; rather, groups may splinter, proliferate, and shift alliances over time. And actions taken against one organization may work in the favor of another. For example, the highly publicized efforts in the 1980s to shut down Colombian drug trade by focusing intense attention on their smuggling routes to the United States via south Florida only succeeded in empowering Mexican traffickers (Andreas 309). Similarly, crackdowns on specific organizations or their leaders, widely diffused via strident media attention, have generally done little to stem the drug trafficking business; when one cartel's hold over a smuggling point diminishes, others simply move in (Andreas 316–17), often in collaboration with corrupt agents of the same enforcement groups that are charged with securitizing the border.

While corruption of Mexican politicians and police authorities has been well documented and is thought to be rampant (Andreas 311–12, 316–17), corruption on the part of US employees within its Border Industrial Complex is by no means rare, either (Andreas 322). Indeed, it might be argued that the larger the security apparatus, the greater the proliferation of potential points of breakdown, infiltration, corruption or collaboration between state border control agencies and illicit commercial merchants.

Borders Don't Exist

Oswaldo Zavala's book *Los cárteles no existen* indeed makes the provocative argument, drawing on the work of numerous experts, that drug cartels, understood as independent criminal syndicates, do not exist as such, at least in accordance with widely disseminated images of their actions and operations, but are better thought of as a construct of the state itself, which "has created a formidable enemy" in them (10). Zavala maintains, "this discursive matrix of the 'narco' originated in the complex binational relationship between Mexico and the United States" (16). Although he does not employ the term, his arguments imply that the Border Industrial Complex itself feeds on the discursive construct of cartels, with all the sensationalized stereotyped images that have emerged around it: "the belief in 'drug cartels' as a new threat to national security was a direct effect of the implementation of a state policy based in part on the conception of a permanent enemy that permits the justification of actions that would otherwise be legal or even immoral" (16). In other words, the notion of "the narco can be reduced to the state's strategies for security" (45).

The idea of the "narco," which has been disseminated most effectively through the entertainment industry, including films, telenovelas, and popular music is, not only according to Zavala but other critics as well, a function of a corrupt government exercising power. In the documentary film, "El guardian de la memoria" (Arteaga), El Paso based attorney Carlos Spector argues that organized crime of the borderlands might be better referred to as "authorized crime": "organized crime cannot exist without the complicity of local, state, and federal government." For Spector, the recent attention to asylum seekers at the border, the vast majority of whose cases are rejected, only serves to hide the ongoing drug related violence along Mexico's northern border. He states, "There is a tacit agreement between the two nations, both of which benefit by playing down the violence," Mexico in terms of media attention, and the US from a bureaucratic perspective. "Impunity permits all of this. Impunity is not a consequence of the violence, but rather the politics of the violence."

Likewise, journalist Anabel Ochoa's book *El traidor* maintains that during Calderón's war on drugs, there were no government officials who resisted the bribes of Joaquín "El Chapo" Guzmán Loera, and that payoffs only increased as his cartel grew stronger. An earlier book, *El cártel incómodo* explains in great detail how El Chapo's organization realized over 40,000 bank transactions involving the business and finance sectors in order to launder money, signaling the deep connections of drug cartels in the private sector on both sides of the border.

For Edgardo Buscaglia, in *Vacíos de poder en México*, precipitous growth in both police and military security along Mexico's northern border has resulted mainly in paradoxical parallel increases in human rights abuses. His investigation exposes the reasons underlying the impunity that has taken ever deeper root in Mexico, underlining the conjecture that narcotics trafficking would not exist without the government.

There is a broad consensus that the border security apparatuses of both the United States and Mexico are deeply entwined with drug trafficking organizations. This includes, following Andreas, not only questions of infiltration or corruption, but also interdependencies that have allowed some narco organizations to gain strength and take over key border smuggling routes once controlled by other groups weakened by border security operatives, and permitted security operations themselves to become ever larger as their highly publicized battles with drug traffickers have fueled the need for ever more muscular security apparatuses. Any conceptualization of a Border Industrial Complex that is conceived in opposition to and not in conjunction with drug trafficking networks may be naïve in taking state discourse on border security too literally, and is thereby likely to misunderstand the complexity of border smuggling and security dynamics. For this reason, we argue here that Mexican drug trafficking operations in Ciudad Juárez, including, as we shall see, the sicario trade within them, are an integral part of the contemporary US-Mexico Border Industrial Complex.

Indeed, it has been argued that state militarization and violence in Mexico directly fed the rise of the sicario trade within drug trafficking organizations in Juárez beginning in the final years of the first decade of the new millennium. In Zavala's view, it is not clear that the business conflict that erupted between the Juárez and the Sinaloa based traffickers in these years would have elicited the same level of violence, the barrage of spectacularized murders, had it not been for the Mexican state's declared "war on drugs." This violent armed conflict dispersed Mexican military units across the country, where they occupied cities and regions targeted as major centers of criminal cartel activity. The campaign, which lasted through the entire six year presidential term of Calderón, employed a rhetoric that echoed the bellicose language that had been in use in the United States for decades, often in support of investing ever more heavily in border militarization (Andreas 175, 311–320). The rise of this "violent militarist strategy" in Mexico, according to Zavala's interpretation, "culminated [...] in the daily horror of Ciudad Juárez" (20). As Andreas notes, Mexico's militarization of its northern border in the Calderón years, with its public takedowns of key leaders and assaults on smuggling routes and mechanisms of cartels dominant at key crossing points, brought about a state of "disorganization, disruption, and competitive scramble to control turf, routes, and market share [that] fueled an unprecedented wave of drug violence in Mexico," which was especially notable in these border cities. Andreas ultimately argues that the sizeable anti-drug trade component of border militarization was deeply collaborative between the two nations: "More than ever before, Mexico and the border became the front line of America's war on drugs" (327).

Indeed, nowhere has this increase in drug related border violence in the new millennium been more palpable than in Ciudad Juárez, a border city deeply connected with its US sister city El Paso (back in the day both were called El Paso del Norte). Like many border cities, they thrive economically due to their mutual proximity and deep commercial and cultural connections. Prior to the mid-1990s, Juárez was reputed to be "a reasonably safe place" (Weissman 824).

BORDER VIOLENCE

A prior wave of violence hit Juárez in the mid 1990s, including a series of highly publicized inadequately investigated and mostly unsolved murders of women that drew worldwide attention to the city. Nonetheless, even with this feminicide scandal, which due to institutional incompetency, indifference or corruption went on for years (see Gaspar de Alva; Monárrez, *Trama*; Valenzuela Arce, *Sed de mal*), Juárez's murder rate was not especially high compared to those of many other Mexican cities until a simmering turf war broke out between the Juárez cartel, which had controlled traffic across the highly profitable Juárez-El Paso border, collecting hefty tolls from other cartels using that route, and the increasingly powerful Sinaloa cartel at the very moment of Calderón's deployment of the Mexican army to Juárez.

Ciudad Juárez is known as a foundational site for Mexico's drug trafficking history, with evidence of an illicit narcotics trade dating back to at least 1906, when it is said that a group of Chinese immigrants fled the earthquake of San Francisco, settling in Juárez, where they established several opium dens (Linares). And while some have called one of them, Sam Hing, the first "capo" (Linares), others designate an organization founded in the 1920s by Pablo "El Pablote" González, who would come to be known as the "csar of morphine," and taken over upon his death in 1931 by his legendary wife Ignacia "La Nacha" Jasso viuda de González, as Mexico's first major narcotics enterprise (Ramírez Pimienta, "El Pablote").

Luis Astorga notes several milestones in the history of the prohibition of what came to be known as narcotics: the 1909 Shanghai Conference at which the United States along with 13 other nations committed to impeding traffic in opium and its derivatives, the precursor to larger global anti-trafficking efforts that would later be led by the United Nations. The 1914 Harrison Act in the US targeted cocaine and opiates, while Mexico's first federal laws that targeted marijuana and poppy based products were enacted in 1920 and 1926. According to Astorga, Mexico's drug trafficking sector was linked to political power from its beginnings, its profitability representing a temptation for politicians, who established mechanisms to protect this growing industry. The experiment of alcohol prohibition in the US (1920–33) served as another catalyst to the development of the narcotics trade at the border.

La Nacha's organization dominated drug trade in Juárez until at least the 1950s, and was superseded by the group that became known as the Juárez cartel by the 1980s (Linares). By this time, Juárez was becoming a major smuggling point into the United States, representing a key site of export for Mexico's "golden triangle," a region of northwestern Mexico, including the states of Chihuahua, Sinaloa and Durango, home to fertile land (for growing marijuana or opium poppies), rugged mountain terrain (well known to locals but difficult for federal or international authorities to surveil) and Ciudad Juárez, Mexico's second busiest commercial and pedestrian crossing point to the United States. For many years, an alliance among various regional cartels (Juárez, Sinaloa, Beltrán Leyva) kept Juárez peaceful. That would change by around 2008.

> *That was when they started to get me in touch with a cousin who had also started working, and he was the one who got in contact with the Sinaloa cartel over there, because in fact we were going to Culiacán, to Durango, we would go to Mazatlán, to Badiraguato, right? We were already moving around there, so they hired us to start shipping cars, new model cars, trucks, around the golden triangle, where we started to meet more people, more people, and we started to aspire to make more money.* (Salmo)

Any notion of collaboration burst apart on the streets of Juárez beginning in 2008. Homicides, nearly all of which could be linked to this turf war, surged from 320 for the year 2007 to 1623 in 2008, 2754 in 2009, and a peak of 3622 in 2010, a period that, as mentioned above, coincided quite precisely with the Mexican federal government's declared "war on drugs," which generated record levels of violence throughout the country, but especially in key transit cities such as Juárez. The industry of illicit drug trafficking did not invest in marketing, lobbying, or customer service in its battle for the control of the Juárez-El Paso border, but rather in murder. And a dramatic increase in demand for murders translated to a similarly sharp upsurge in demand for murderers, laying out a lucrative career track for a generation of young men—and, very rarely, women—of the Juárez-El Paso borderlands, of which Salmo, took advantage.

The violence of golden triangle drug trade was not new, although this region's prominence as a major center of the borderland drug industry was less well known to many than some other sites, such as Tamaulipas, where a syndicate initially known as the Matamoros Cartel, later the Gulf Cartel, had been visibly active for decades (see Padgett). For example, a major location for the illicit drug business, Badiraguato, Sinaloa, was largely ignored for years by Mexican and international media due to its small size (population of only a few thousand) and remoteness—though Badiraguato would later gain prominence as the birthplace, and for many years headquarters, of Joaquín Guzmán Loera, better known as "El Chapo," the now legendary capo of the Sinaloa cartel. The northern Sierra Madre Occidental mountain region of Sinaloa, Durango and Chihuahua has a long history of cultivation of marijuana and opium poppy. Its more remote and sparsely populated regions became known, especially in recent decades, for being independent of control of law enforcement, and rife with drug related crime. However, a high murder rate and significant and open cartel activity in a small town or in a rural county doesn't translate to media visibility. Nor does a high murder rate there signify an alarmingly large number of murders in absolute terms.

Juárez was different. It is a big city, a regional industrial center, a major hub of crossborder shipping. The rapid rise of its murder rate due to conflicts within the drug trafficking sector transformed the image of the city. It not only drew worldwide attention to drug trafficking activities, but it also highlighted a lucrative career path within that sector. With paid assassinations numbering in the thousands each year, as was the case from 2008 through 2012, many young men in the Juárez border region found opportunities that they might otherwise never have seen as sicarios.

We should make clear that much of the violence attributed to the drug cartels in Juárez between 2008 and 2012 was carried out not by the core personnel of the cartels themselves, but by affiliated organizations. La Línea, for example, is known as "the armed enforcement wing of the Juárez cartel" (Dávila 42), and has its own affiliate gangs in Ciudad Juárez, including, prominently, los Aztecas, which had been known as the main street dealing network in the city, operating at one point six thousand *picaderos* (drug dens or shooting galleries—points of retail sales) there; then when Juárez became a battlefield around 2008, "La Línea turned them into their army of sicarios" (Dávila 45).

Job Markets, Career Paths

We started working in that line from 2008, from the beginning of the massacre, always here. We went around and now we saw all the massacres that were going on here, you know, from 2008 when all the assassinations started in Ciudad Juárez, right? 2008, 2009 and 2010 [...] No, I wasn't so deeply involved in that, right? I only took part in driving the truck. Then after a bit, how long? maybe three years ago, or four, is when I began to get involved, now for real, more fully. (Salmo)

Not all drug smugglers or thieves of course are cut out to be assassins. However, since the rise of the narcocorrido, in the 1970s and 1980s, narcoviolence had been romanticized, with the golden triangle region frequently located at the heart of it all. Chalino Sánchez, a hugely popular corrido recording artist from Sinaloa, did not specialize in narcocorridos, but did compose and sing them. And his own personal history of violence—including his putative move from Sinaloa to the US to escape prosecution or retribution for a murder, his own involvement in a shootout at one of his concerts, and finally his unsolved murder upon returning to Sinaloa for a concert—by the time of his death in 1992, was very firmly linked, through his much admired public persona, to drug trafficking and violence via a romanticized association with masculine honor and valor (Ramírez Pimienta). While Sánchez's personal story certainly did not understate the risks involved in narcoviolence, it did bring it to the mainstream, and make it clear that it was an option for ambitious individuals thinking about potentially glamorous career options in crime.

In the case of Salmo, it appears that after discovering the option of crossborder crime as a way to make easy money, he was drawn to the more lucrative options in the illicit drug industry. This led him to gradually enter into it more deeply, eventually becoming an accomplice to assassinations, and finally an assassin himself. While it is possible that he might have become a killer had he grown up somewhere else, the multiple criminal options evident to a young Salmo in the borderlands perhaps tempted him more than they might have elsewhere, and in places with lower murder rates, becoming a paid assassin might never have come to mind. But Salmo grew up in the borderlands, the borderlands drug trade drew him in, and the war on drugs offered work opportunities in killing.

He insists that this was not his only option. Many other intrepid borderlands kids might have opted to cross undocumented into the United

States and try their luck there. And many others might have taken career paths achievable through education more seriously. While many young people in Juárez have ended up working long hours for meager pay, sometimes subjected to abuse and exploitation, in the city's large maquiladora industry or other low paying sectors, the labor market in Juárez, with historically lower unemployment rates and higher pay rates than those seen in many other parts of Mexico, was in the early 2000s reasonably robust by Mexican standards. Salmo makes clear that he was not forced into any decisions due to economic urgency.

> *They gave us everything, in fact, my parents never failed to provide for me, I never felt a lack of affection, nothing. I mean, they gave me everything, but the simple fact is that I got into it out of curiosity, right? And because I started getting ambitious with money, you know?*

While Salmo did come from a humble background, he does not describe his family as having been desperately poor, and does not seem to have felt hopeless. But the borderland drug trafficking industry beckoned him and drew him in, just around the time that Juárez was becoming the most violent city in the world.

Other investigations on sicarios construct a somewhat different scenario. One study claims that young people are recruited by the cartels directly as sicarios, that is, they do not work their way up the ranks, but rather are hired directly as killers, which is their sole area of specialization. It also asserts that these young people choose to become assassins "as an alternative to resolve their economic situation" (Corvero Quevedo and Lara Ruiz 67). Others argue that some may be threatened or otherwise obliged to become assassins, with economic enticements used to keep them motivated and loyal (*Norte Digital* 11/2/2014: https://nortedigital.mx/la-desgarradora-historia-de-un-nino-sicario/). There are, to be sure, well known cases of sicarios being "coerced" into the trade (Langton 232–33), sometimes by means as extreme as kidnapping (Langton 210). However, it is notable that neither Salmo, nor any of our other interviewees, claimed to have been forced to kill, nor did they portray their work as sicarios as disconnected from other job lines within drug trafficking hierarchies.

One investigation argues in a discussion focusing in part on the participation of minors in paid assassinations, "cartels were outsourcing their criminal tasks, including assassinations, to youngsters" (Langton 112). Without a doubt the recruiting of youth in the role of sicarios was, unfortunately, common, at least during the height of violence in Juárez. However, regarding the issues of the relationship of sicarios to the cartels, that is, whether they are freelance pay for hire assassins or rank and file salaried employees, the same investigation, in citing interviews with a fourteen year old sicario, known as "El Ponchis," whose arrest drew intense media attention in 2010, notes that after this young man was initially "kidnapped" by the organization known as the Beltrán Leyva cartel, he "had worked for them ever since, with a starting salary of $2,500 a murder" (233), indicating that he was not a free agent working on commission, but rather a salaried employee of the business.

Furthermore, and perhaps in contrast with the highly publicized case cited above, while all of those interviewed for this study admitted to having participated in paid assassinations, none seemed to think of themselves specifically as sicarios—all were narcos who had engaged in robbery, kidnapping, drug smuggling, drug dealing, assault, or other criminal activities among which murder was one. It was one that left an important mark on their conscience, but someone like Salmo was ultimately no more or less an assassin than he was a smuggler or a thief: he was all of those things as all were positions he held, initially as a freelancer, then later as part of the industrial infrastructure of the drug trafficking business.

Salmo's experience as a freelancer was that of larceny and smuggling, and his initial participation in the narcotrafficking industry was in larceny and smuggling. He might well have maintained those same areas of specialization had the business disagreement between the Juárez and Sinaloa cartels not turned to violence. If the Sinaloa cartel had not elected to increase its commissions for murders in Ciudad Juárez tenfold, it would have had no need to transform its salaried thieves and smugglers into salaried killers. Indeed, it is likely that the latter is a job at which not all thieves and smugglers would excel, nor would all of them want to take it on. Therefore, during the period of what Salmo calls "the massacre" (2008–2012), he receives a significant increase in salary and benefits for his work as a sicario:

They now gave us something, a salary, a salary and … it was good, it was well paid and besides that, there were many privileges for us to do what we wanted, right?

SALARYMEN

It is important to note that Salmo refers specifically to earning a "salary"; Salmo was never a freelance assassin, was never paid strictly by commission for any killing. He was not a casual and independent participant in a loosely structured network of crime and violence. Rather he was an employee whose compensation, including a generous salary—and "privileges," on which he doesn't elaborate, but which might be thought of as fringe benefits—was paid through the corporate infrastructure of the cartel that employed him; he was a prominent corporate player in Juárez's Border Industrial Complex.

His motivations to take on what was clearly a prestigious but not necessarily coveted job within the cartel included the money, which is what had originally drawn him to this career path, but also the excitement and the power he felt from carrying out this labor. Speaking of his involvement with the cartel and his work as assassin, Salmo explains:

> We started to aspire to make more money and now began to enjoy the ... the adrenaline that we felt [...] Now we, as they say, exerted authority, we – my brother, may he rest in peace, and I – were now the most fearsome men of the neighborhood, right?

It was a career path of high risk, and high rewards. And the benefit of prestige was especially attractive and satisfying.

Unfortunately for Salmo's brother, the high risk apparently got him killed. And while Salmo was lucky enough to avoid that fate, he did end up imprisoned, with a one year sentence in the Centro de Reinserción Social (CERESO) prison in Ciudad Juárez for drug trafficking.

SHIFTING PROFESSIONAL PRIORITIES, PERSONAL REDEMPTION

While Salmo does not give a specific timeline, he does state that his involvement with the Sinaloa cartel coincided with the period he calls "the massacre," and it can be inferred that by the time he was released from prison, cartel killings had dropped significantly. The peak year for Juárez homicides was 2010 (3622), with the number of killings going below 1000 by 2012 and reduced to only about 300 by 2014. Undoubtedly, this translated to a drying up of the labor market for paid assassins.

When Salmo left prison, he prioritized reuniting with his family, which he had abandoned for four years:

> *Thank God I found them, struggling, struggling. But so far what I've realized is that … well, I'm a very different person, right? in comparison with my past life. I now feel that my life, that my wife, now … she really feels secure, she feels supported by me […] Well, now, the truth is that the massacre in Juárez has dropped off a bit. The crime, well … like everything, right? there's crime everywhere, but now organized crime's role has diminished, to what it was like years ago, yes it's diminished.*

Salmo makes clear that he was not pressured to return to his old job as sicario upon his release from prison, and that he felt free to return to his family and establish a different kind of lifestyle, away from the cartel.

Salmo's imprisonment blurs the line of interpretation regarding his separation from his employer. Salmo wished to leave, and ceased to participate, an instance of what nowadays might be called ghosting: leaving a job without formally resigning. On the other hand, with demand for assassinations significantly reduced, the cartel might have preferred to lay him off. His separation, then, seems to have occurred via a tacit agreement. Salmo interprets his choice to return to his family as something of which his former employers actually approve:

> *So far when I've run into people I used to work with, they've greeted me and I've told them I'm seeking the way of God. And they've told me "go for it, go for it," contrary to what you might think … It's not like "you join the mafia and can never get out", right? In our case, where I was, it was like your family or the gang, and if you embrace your family, there's no problem, "go ahead, just get yourself together."*

In this way, Salmo found an exit and sought redemption for his past deeds, and a peaceful and upright life for the future. In other words, he makes clear that he does not see himself as a sort of natural born killer, an inherently bad hombre, but rather someone who committed some misdeeds. He admits that his acts of violence were serious and perhaps morally indefensible, but he has found a way to move on and live a life far removed from delinquency and the dangers that his old life brought upon him. His work as a sicario was, in the end, not a professional calling, but labor; it was the role he played in the industry for a few years. Now he has moved on to another phase of his personal and professional life. Luckily for him:

The truth of the matter is that for all the damage we did, in my case, what I did, God has already forgiven me; he's already forgiven me for everything.

THE CASE OF TONY

Tony's story, as outlined below, echoes many of the same themes as that of Salmo, including his personal history (humble background, but not one of abject poverty), his induction into organized crime (through crossborder smuggling), and his professional ambitions within the Border Industrial Complex (aspirations related to both money and prestige). Tony makes clear that he had many other opportunities in life that might have brought him economic security and personal satisfaction far removed from the drug trafficking business:

I'm Mexican via my parents, but was born over in the United States [...], dual nationality [...] I spent my childhood here, right here in Ciudad Juárez, here in Mexico. I went to the United States after junior high, that was when I did high school over there in the United States, and that was when my whole story began, right?, with organized crime.

Tony grew up with the privilege of US citizenship, even though he didn't live there until he was a teenager. He then went to live with his grandparents, on his father's side, who resided in El Paso, while his parents were in the process of obtaining their own green cards, which were approved soon afterwards. Tony, as a US citizen, had access not only to US public high school, but would also be eligible to study in US universities, which would imply the right to reduced in-state tuition in Texas, and financial aid, including federal grants and loans.

As a student ... well, I was a good student. [...] I always got good grades. Really ... the atmosphere ... when you go from here in Mexico to the United States, especially at a difficult age, well there's a lot of bullying, that's what happened ... I started to be a rebel, to get into trouble, into fights. But that's how it is [...] Well, ever since I was a kid I was into sports, I was an athlete [...] But my childhood actually was a little difficult due to the change in environment, from here in Mexico to the United States, and that's when I started to get involved with the wrong people, as they say [...]

Tony did finish high school "very much by force," and as a teen had no trouble finding work "at McDonalds, at Whataburger, all that." And he did actually try to pursue a college education, but got waylaid as he became involved in criminal activities. Tony, then, like Salmo, was not forced to become a sicario due to a profound or urgent financial need. Indeed, he could presumably have earned a college degree that would have led him quite possibly to a comfortable middle class status in the United States. Drug trafficking was one of many possible career paths he might have chosen.

It should be noted that despite the idea of drug cartels being labeled always as Mexican, their heightened activity along the border often invites participation of US citizens of the borderlands. One especially famous case is that of Edgar Valdez Villarreal, better known as "el Barbie," a capo of the Beltrán Leyva organization, who was born and raised in Laredo, Texas, and who, like Tony, began his career as a petty criminal, eventually being recruited into a cartel, where he rose up through the ranks (Langton 197). Another is that of the juvenile sicario, cited above, who was born and raised in San Diego, but moved to Mexico when his parents were deported, falling into criminal activities after dropping out of school "after third grade," and eventually getting recruited to a the Pacífica Sur cartel, which later trained him as a sicario (Langton 232).

Sicarios as Border Thinkers

Tony's biographical trajectory signals the importance of the border in his process of growing up and learning about the world. He crossed not only between Mexico and the US, Spanish and English, but between school and street, college and cartel. As exotic as Tony's work may seem, his background was ordinary: no personal history of extreme poverty, or extreme domestic violence, or extreme child abuse. Tony's very ordinary life experience prior to his induction into organized crime makes him potentially a "border thinker" (Mignolo), who can translate his not very ordinary life as a paid assassin in terms that can be widely understood on the other side, in sectors far removed from drug violence.

Tony recalls:

> *I started getting involved with people who offered easy money, right? That's when I got into it and started everything, I mean getting involved with all kinds of people, with people who you can't imagine meeting.*

Not only is Tony's personal history one of the borderlands as a "third space," (Dear) in which he belonged to both nations, yet not really to either one, but also his life from adolescence on was defined by border crossing and cultural clashes, and by the distinct work opportunities within the industry of drug trafficking.

> *They started off using me as, using me as they say, as a mule, here in the United States, in El Paso, receiving all the shipments, all the drug shipments, ... to assure that they went right, that they all arrived complete, without anything missing, right? And from there, well I rose up in the organization [...] And they keep an eye on your limits: how far can you go, how far are you willing to go, how high you want to rise.*

Tony, like Salmo, was not a freelance killer, but rather was part of "the organization." Nor was he a specialist in murder from day one; rather he started off working in drug smuggling, and eventually elected to work his way up a particular path on the corporate cartel ladder.

He explains the industrial pay structure for his own labor as a sicario:

> *An organization, yes ..., they give you your pay for the event, and if not, whether you do it or not you get your weekly salary.*

Put another way, like Salmo, Tony received a salary as an employee of the cartel, but also would earn bonus pay for carrying out specific violent acts. He elaborates further:

> *There's a moment in which they ask you for something specific, whether someone stole something, or because ... for a finger, right? They ask you "You know what, bro, we need you to cut off a finger, a hand, a leg, and to leave something written so that they realize that this organization doesn't get played, and that this is a serious thing," right? But yes, yes, there are some heavy assignments, and special assignments, which, yes, are also paid. It depends on how important the person is.*

More routine tasks are covered by a weekly salary, while others, particularly targeted assassinations, would also warrant payment by event.

Tony's motivations in joining a cartel and, later, becoming a sicario were similar to those of Salmo: not dire need, but rather the attraction of easy money and "the partying." He echoes Salmo's thrill at "the adrenaline." In addition, he avers:

It was [...] making a name for yourself, I mean ... you believe you're Superman.
That says it all – you think you're king of the world.

CROSSING BACK

Tony, like Salmo, ended up in jail. But unlike Salmo, who performed all of his labor in his later years in the cartel in Ciudad Juárez, and ended up incarcerated in Mexico, Tony was imprisoned in Texas:

> *I was jailed for five years, and in those five years, well, as they say, you learn a*
> *lot more because you meet more people inside; you hang out more with people*
> *from other countries, from other states, from other cities. And, well, like they say,*
> *it's a little school, right?*

While Tony doesn't go into any more detail regarding the role of Mexican drug cartels in US prisons, his view of prison as a kind of school coincides with those of several other sicarios interviewed for this project, including Alberto, who claims to have learned his criminal trade in prison, and Anastasio, who was recruited into the Sinaloa cartel while doing time at the CERESO prison in Juárez in 2009.

Like Salmo, Tony sought to get out of organized crime upon leaving prison, completing a vocational program to become certified as a medical assistant. However, his life plans were thwarted when he realized that his criminal record prevented him from being hired for the kinds of jobs he sought in the United States, while his US degree was meaningless in Mexico, where the occupation of medical assistant does not exist. He therefore reverted to criminal activities.

> *When I got out, I thought, well, that I'd go straight. I started studying to be a*
> *medical assistant and I finished fine, but here in Mexico the degree is worthless.*
> *I mean, here you can be either a doctor or a nurse, only, and studies from over*
> *there don't mean anything. So I struggled a lot because of my criminal record*
> *there in the United States [...] For drugs, for conspiracy, for distribution, those*
> *were the charges against me [...] Unfortunately, when you have a criminal*
> *record, you get out, you want to have a normal life, and you can't because they*
> *see you as a criminal, they don't give you a second chance, which is why I went*
> *back to the same thing. I couldn't get a job, I couldn't get a job [...], so I went*
> *back to the same thing, I went back to the same thing, until I dropped down*
> *lower than I ever thought I would. I got into trouble again, and that's why I'm*
> *here now in Mexico.*

Incarceration allowed Tony to get out of the drug trade—again, it is likely that while doing jail time, the demand for specialized work in murder fell as a relative peace returned to Juárez, which allowed him to spend a few years clean, studying, without being threatened or harassed. It was actually only when he realized he couldn't find work in the field of his degree on either side of the border that he went back to criminal activities—he doesn't say what they were this time—on his own initiative. However, it is likely that by the time he got out, and certainly by the time he went back to Mexico, his services as paid assassin were no longer necessary. The spike in murders was just for a few years, after which being a full time professional murderer was no longer an option for many within the Ciudad Juárez narcotics industry.

> I've heard a statistic that there were more deaths here in Juárez than in Afghanistan, in the Afghanistan war. But now at this moment, no. Not so many are being reported because … it's still the same, still the same, but now it's more like, as they say, more … silenced. Because there are still lots of murders, I can say over turf, right?, for market control – there's always going to be conflict here over the market. Because this is a borderland: here's where all the dough, all the money is. That's why they want to take control of the market. But to say it's calming down, or that it's going to calm down … well, that would be hard.

While Tony believes there are still a lot of murders in Juárez (by 2019, the annual toll had risen back to nearly 1500), it's not likely that 3000 of them are going unreported or are being kept out of the public eye. The cartels may still be at it, but the intensity has gone down, and no one has been on his back to go back to his old job.

In fact, he states that, like Salmo, he feels free to go about his life, and that he's not under threat at all. He feels no "fear […] that I owe something, or that they're looking for me, no, no." Being a sicario during the surge in violence of Ciudad Juárez does not imply being a sicario for life, nor does it seem even to constitute a realistic option for long term steady employment.

Furthermore, despite his previous bout of recidivism, Tony appears to no longer have any interest in returning to those activities. He in fact claims to regret his exploits as a salaried assassin, although he often believed he was killing people who "deserved" what they were getting: "Yes, I'm sorry for a lot of things, but only he from beyond can judge me. He decides the degree of seriousness [of my sins] when I leave here." In fact, in contrast with the idea of underlying securitization discourse in both the United States and Mexico (which is often echoed by those who write about the narcotics industry, including many of the authors cited in this chapter, such as Michael Dear), Tony's view of drug trafficking organizations is not completely negative; they do not represent for him the pure evil implied by their image as purveyors of criminality and violence. He advocates a more nuanced view of Mexican cartels:

> *An organization, if it's criminal, there are various divisions: drug trafficking, kidnapping, extortion, and even murder, when they need a sicario, right? [...] I've been in all kinds of categories, you know, but when they say that organized crime is only death, in reality they're not seeing beyond the violence that harms people, makes people look bad, all of that. They don't see the good side, how they help the community, how they provide support for friends that might be in jail now, you know? who can't take care of their families – out here they can count on getting economic support.*

Family support while incarcerated would seem to be a fringe benefit, not unlike medical or disability benefits provided to state employees. While none of this is written into formal contracts or employee handbooks, drug trafficking organizations offer some employment perks analogous to those that employees working in other industries within the Border Industrial Complex might receive.

Some Observations

The cases of Tony and Salmo share a few elements that challenge some widespread notions regarding sicarios and their livelihoods. Neither one of them reports being pressured into becoming a sicario, or facing extreme limits on work options. Both admit to choosing organized crime despite knowing they had other possibilities, both signaling ways in which the border itself, as a lucrative site of smuggling, helped lure them into lives of crime and violence. Neither one identifies specifically as a sicario; both rather tell of performing multiple jobs as they followed a career path within the organization that employed them. And both left freely, suffering no repercussions for abandoning the organization. It remains to be seen whether the huge psychological repercussions of their work as sicarios, which they struggle to justify and to put behind them, will allow them to see themselves in a positive light and to lead productive nonviolent lives in the long run. But the two cited here are making a go of it. Their experience as sicarios, then, marks but does not define them; it is a path they chose for a few years, and later came to regret, a consequence of their location within the Border Criminal Industrial Complex at a moment of heightened violence.

CHAPTER 3

Youthful Murderers: Innocence and Professionalism

On February 26, 2019, the Mexican news media published a story about a 16 year old who, with the help of a friend, murdered his parents, put their bodies into black garbage bags, and tossed them into a vacant lot near their house in the town of Yahuatepec, Morelos, in central Mexico. It is notable the killer initially called the police to report the disappearance of his parents, but as the investigation got underway, he began contradicting himself in his declarations. Once the evidence started adding up against him, he confessed. One of the admissions of the killer, who as a juvenile was sentenced to a maximum of five years of confinement, was that the double homicide (patricide) was part of a recruitment test of a criminal group (Méndez).

Approaching Mexican Youth

Writing about youth is a complex task as the passage of time has a significant impact on this age group that, as a moving target, is difficult to define. While there may be differences across different social settings—for example, urban versus rural, wealthy versus impoverished—there are some factors that seem to present similar risks across demographics. There are now several decades of studies on youth in Mexico that approach young people from diverse perspectives, although it seems that the most recurrent preoccupation within this body of research is the role of the neoliberal system. For example, scholar activist Rossana Reguillo proposes several different ways that neoliberalism as a dominant socioeconomic project employs biopolitics as means of appropriation of young bodies through processes that she provocatively calls "decapitalizations" (*Emergencia* 43). Along these same lines, Maritza Urteaga Castro Pozo draws attention to the stagnation of the Mexican state over the past five decades and the consequent impact on basic rights, giving rise to new forms of experiencing youth (27). José Manuel Valenzuela Arce sustains that the neoliberal model that has spread throughout Latin America has left marked effects of inequality that are especially pronounced among youth ("Identidades" 21). In his studies of youth groups, he finds that perceptions of a destructive capitalism inspire a battle cry among some young people, whose position is summed up as: "We are not anti-system, the system is anti-us" ("Las voces" 30).

Applying Zygmunt Bauman's metaphor, the lives of young people in Mexico could be understood as "liquid" (see his *Liquid Modernity*), as economic norms have not been capable of resolving or compensating for the market's inability to distribute wealth in a more equitable way, and thereby protect them from labor precarity and pauperization. Due in part to limited options—as well as bad decision making when confronted with the crisis in basic social infrastructure: failing schools, weak labor markets, poor healthcare, and sometimes dysfunctional families, a major sector of young people is currently at risk of dying young. Drug trafficking can be thought of as a locomotive that has the power to pull, carry, and drag off anyone who gets on board, in at least two ways: either through recruitment to the ranks of a criminal organization, or enticement by the same organizations as a customer, a drug user who may become and addict and a public health problem. Drug trafficking constantly takes the lives of young people in Mexico on both tracks.

Figures offer insight into the current situation for youth in Mexico. The presidency of Felipe Calderón Hinojosa (2006–2012) registered 121,613 homicides, a count rising during that of Enrique Peña Nieto (2012–2018) to 156,437—a total of 278,050 during those 12 years, of which 90% were male, and 40% between ages 12 and 29 (Carolina and Adrián), an equivalent during those 12 years of 45 young men murdered per day. The war on drugs in Mexico has entailed a profound change in social structures: "The statistics and discourses that circulate in the public sphere seem to indicate that there is an excess population of youth that is perceived as dispensable and often as the cause of social problems"

(Ruvalcaba and Ravelo 63). Being young in many places is a greater risk factor for death than illness. Furthermore, the majority of protagonists in the violence against youth are other youth.

While the righteous case against violence itself is not up for debate, the participation of young people in violence, as well as its impact on them, presents ethical dilemmas. Violence is assumed not to be inherent to mankind, but rather of men's (and not women's) creation, most often explained through cultural structures. The question of how much responsibility to assign to young people for violent acts is difficult, as well as whether these violent behaviors are best addressed by education or punishment. Likewise, legal dividing lines whether by age or by level of violence, between juveniles and adults are inevitably arbitrary approximations. Young people who have committed extreme acts of violence for example, sicarios—may offer helpful insights into debates on these questions. Their testimonial narratives point to criteria that they themselves may use in separating youthful innocence from adult accountability.

INNOCENCE AND RESPONSIBILITY

There are many scenarios for which societies distinguish between minors and adults in assigning social responsibilities (e.g., requirements to serve in armed forces), in sanctioning privileges (voting, driving a car, drinking alcohol), or in holding individuals accountable for their acts (consensual sexual acts) based on approximations of when a young person is thought to have become mature enough to understand the complexities of adult life and take make judicious decisions. These arbitrary dividing lines are often set in absolute terms, much like height restrictions for certain rides at amusement parks. Either young people make the cut, or they don't, generally based not on psychological evaluations, but on date of birth.

The same applies to criminal justice systems, which often exclude juveniles, usually defined by age, who are thought to be too young to be held accountable and punished as adults for certain acts. For example, the United States Supreme Court has ruled that "juvenile offenders are less culpable than adults because: (1) they are less able to assess risk; (2) they are more susceptible to outside influences; and (3) they do not have a fully developed character" (Kellogg 267). While age limits separating youth from adulthood vary from place to place, and from context to context— cutoffs may be at 16, 18, 21—they tend to be set at the end of the teen years or the onset of the twenties, although some experts have argued in the case of criminal justice for raising the limit to as high as age 24 (Loeber, et al. 20–21).

Meanwhile, school age individuals, considered by many to be children, have increasingly become involved in criminal drug trafficking organizations, often sophisticated groups that collectively engage in very adult style criminal violence. These organizations may recruit young people for certain high exposure roles in smuggling or drug dealing. But they have also increasingly recruited young people, school age children, and trained them to carry out violent acts, including murder. Juveniles who remain in school will usually be treated as children, but the same school age children who become professional assassins may be viewed differently. Sicarios themselves may themselves adopt criteria assigning innocence to some young people but not to others based not on their age or their maturity, but on their acts.

> *Yeah, those were our orders: to not kill innocents; we didn't kill women or children, unless the woman was the target, only then, but we didn't kill innocent women or children who had nothing to do* [with drug trafficking]. (Anastasio)

Notably, in the context described above, while women and children who were not involved in the drug trade were thought of as innocent, no such qualifier is offered for men. However, in the above comment, Anastasio does not clarify what determines whether someone is a child, who may or may not be considered "innocent," and a man, who implicitly does not seem to qualify to be spared for this reason, even if he is a bystander who has nothing to do with organized crime.

Educational attrition has long been a serious problem in north central Mexico. In the 2013–2014 school year a total of 26,757 students dropped out of high school in the state of Chihuahua alone, putting the state in "first place in the country in high school dropout rates" (*El Diario* 7/30/2014: https://diario.mx/Local/2014-07-30_9938a36a/chihuahua-primer-lugar-del-pais-por-desercion-en-prepas/). This problem extends beyond high school as more recent data indicates that in the 2018–2019 school year, roughly 25,000 children who completed elementary school never registered for junior high school because they didn't see it as an "attractive" option (*El Diario* 10/14/2019: https://diario.mx/juarez/25-mil-dejan-la-secundaria-porque-no-les-atrae-20191013-1574314.html). Regardless of the state of the job market, the earlier young people drop out of school, the more limited their employment options in adulthood. Although it should be noted that some decisions to drop out might be the result of young people being forced to take on adult responsibilities.

> *So from like fifteen, fourteen on, you're not a kid anymore. You move on, like there are no more children. I mean there are young people, there are young people that don't get into this, right? But, yeah, from fourteen on, not anymore.* (Anastasio)

In his much cited text *After Violence*, Johan Galtung, a specialist in peace and conflict studies, argues that visible violence is preceded by structural violence, that is, an underlying conflict that does not let up with any possible solution to the crisis of violence, but rather becomes embedded as cultural violence. To assume that structural violence is not at play in Mexico would be a catastrophic mistake. Crime rates and homicide statistics in Mexico from the first half of the twentieth century are surprisingly high by contemporary standards. "For many years, Mexico registered elevated levels of homicide. From 1931 to 1954, there were 257,000 cases" (Wolfgang and Ferracutti, 298). Although the figures may not be strictly comparable over time, it is worth considering per capita data, taking into account Mexico's population of approximately 16.5 million and 26 million in 1931 and 1954, respectively, and the 2015 level of 119,938 million (INEGI). To be clear, from 1931 to 1954, Mexico's homicide rate was roughly five per 100,000 inhabitants, while from 2006 to 2018, the figure had fallen to less than half that.

In referring to violence, Galtung seeks to establish a before and an after; part of the thesis of his book is that in the process of moving from "before violence" to "violence," serious implications emerge concerning structure and culture (32). Although the 2006–12 war on drugs might be considered a transition period with regard to this violence, Juárez had already been well known worldwide for a trend of violence that began to develop in the 1990s, a phenomenon that came to be known first as "the Juárez deaths" and later as the city's "feminicides." Together with the adjustments in the drug trafficking scene of the city following the death of the Juárez cartel's founding figure and leader, Amado Carrillo Fuentes in 1997, this recent history makes it difficult to identify a specific "before the violence" or to define a period of violence itself, in Juárez. Both antecedents point instead to elements of structural violence. The official war on drugs, which began in 2006 in line with then president Felipe Calderón's official discourse, and echoed in the media, soon zeroed in on Ciudad Juárez as the most dangerous city in the world, inspiring headlines such as "41 Die in Four Days in Juárez Killing Spree, Official Says" (CNN 4/5/2011: http://edition.cnn.com/2011/WORLD/americas/04/05/mexico. juarez.killings/index.html), with the annual homicide rate for the city rising as high as 229 per 100,000 inhabitants. For many experts on juvenile crime, a context of deep structural violence is likely to lead to greater levels of delinquency among impressionable minors.

UNDERGROUND DEVELOPMENTS

In my unit, the youngest was thirteen, a thirteen year old minor was a sicario.
He was addicted to killing people, that kid really enjoyed killing people. And in
fact right now he's incarcerated, waiting for his trial. (Anastasio)

Julia Monárrez argues that Ciudad Juárez became a site for the industrialization of death through widely diffused disturbing images of bloody cadavers, and elevated death statistics. Biological or cultural bodies: body parts, quartered bodies, identified and unidentified remains, skeletons, the disappeared all signal a society in social crisis, a crisis of violence. Following Achille Mbembe she argues that Juárez experienced "the culmination of a process of the dehumanization and the industrialization of death" (quoted in "Ciudad Juárez" 207), exposing what she calls "underground developments," making evident cultural tendencies that were not new, but in fact had been brewing for decades (Monárrez, "Ciudad Juárez" 207).

The structural violence in Juárez can be understood through a historical framework: the city's important role in the Mexican revolution of the 1910s; the effervescence and exploitation of the city as a huge bar, a role it assumed prominently with the prohibition of alcohol in the United States from 1920 to 1933; the Mexican norm permitting alcohol consumption beginning at 18 rather than 21 years of age, and its proximity to Fort Bliss, a US military base in El Paso that grew significantly during the cold war, and has long lured young men across the border in search of nightlife and prostitution; and also the foundation of the first criminal groups dedicated to narcotics sales (dating at least to the mid-1920s), including those of the legendary Nacha (Ignacia Jasso) and later the Juárez cartel, with the Carrillo Fuentes family contributing particular dynamics. The over 500 feminicides of the 1990s, and the later outbreak of violence among rival drug trafficking groups, led into the Mexican war on drugs, whose end was officially declared only in 2019 by Mexican president Andrés Manuel López Obrador; nonetheless high rates of violent crime have continued, eliciting frequent travel alerts from the US due to the perceived high risk of simply being in Ciudad Juárez.

The choices that young people make in getting involved in the drug trade may be complex, as Tony describes below. He recognizes here—not making a specific link to his work as a sicario—that drugs corrupt youth, but also emphasizes that drug trafficking organizations may offer means to help out young people who are not able to turn to family or to private or public services to meet basic needs.

> *It's evil if you involve people in bad faith, but if you do it to help out people who need it, even if it's a good deed, yes, it's still organized crime. Selling drugs, you know, does great damage to many innocent people, including children, right? But if you have the awareness of helping people who really need it, this means that you were trying to help.* (Tony)

The apparent lack of coherence in his expression here perhaps signals the complexity of the context, or his difficulties in justifying his own acts of violence. Initially he says that any "good deed" carried out by an organized criminal syndicate is still criminal, if not "evil." However, he wants to redeem criminal acts carried out with good intentions. Organized crime, with all its bloodshed, offered him an opportunity, which he used to help himself and also to help his loved ones. Nonetheless, it is hard to condone a situation in which these kinds of decisions—whether or not to kill, whether a homicide is somehow justifiable—are being made by teenagers.

The "underground developments" described by Monárrez are those ruptures from which large social and economic differences emerge in some sectors of the population. For many sociologists, they are the insterstices of social inequality and poverty. The crisis of violence in recent years has been the culmination of a series of factors that together might be understood as a structural "juvenicide," in which basic social networks of the most vulnerable segments of the population go adrift and are unable to develop. José Manuel Valenzuela Arce considers juvenicide an extreme, in which sectors of specific groups of the youth population are subject to being murdered. However, he emphasizes that this social violence should be defined not only by death, but also by the processes leading to economic and social precarization (Valenzuela, *Juvenicidio*).

Tony again emphasizes the role of organized crime in meeting community needs by making possible redistributions of wealth:

> *I truly don't regret what I've done because in terms of good and evil I've known good people, people who have also suffered since they were born, through all of their childhood, into their youth, and that I've helped however I can, in giving them some affection and support, like a brother or even a father would.* (Tony)

No Future

The heartbreaking scene of a father sobbing and embracing the lifeless body of his young son in the street, crying "my son, my son," was published by major communications media throughout Mexico in early 2019. The father of the youth wept inconsolably in a hard to watch scene that contrasted with the larger story. The boy lying dead was 16 years old, and had robbed customers of a food concession at gunpoint in Ecatepec, Mexico State. He was shot down in the act by police officers. Minutes later, the father came upon the tragic scene creating this jarring media image. Soon after that, the boy's brother, also very young, arrived shouting threats at the police on the scene. In the following days, the brother posted videos on social media swearing that he would get revenge by killing the police who had taken the life of his brother (Infobae 7/24/2019: https://www.infobae.com/america/mexico/2019/07/24/eddie-tenia-16-anos-cuando-murio-al-asaltar-un-negocio-en-edomex-sus-amigos-lo-despiden-con-disparos-de-metralletas-y-dicen-que-se-vengaran/). Two weeks later both brother and father were arrested under warrants for robbery. News media indicated that both belonged to a local criminal group known as the "Cabezones" (Infobae 8/1/2019: https://www.infobae.com/america/mexico/2019/08/01/el-padre-que-lloro-a-su-hijo-adolescente-abatido-tras-un-robo-fue-detenido-junto-con-otro-de-sus-hijos-tenian-antecedentes-penales/).

Aspirations for growth through employment often play out across a country like Mexico with pronounced inequality, with palpable effects on many young people. In Ciudad Juárez, manufacturing is the largest employment sector, with the vast majority of investment in the sector coming from abroad. Factory work generally implies a 48 hour work week for a way of 1200–1400 pesos, which translates to 60 or 70 US dollars. A comparable salary, but often with fewer benefits, might be obtained working in a nonprofessional office job, or an informal business. Meanwhile, the weekly earnings of a sicario might run in the range of 4000 to 7000 pesos, or 200 to 350 dollars, for many fewer hours of labor. Criminal groups are well known to actively recruit young people from the city's most vulnerable neighborhoods, although there is no statistical data to gauge what number or proportion of youth respond and take up this career path. However, the scenario above suggests that they may join not only due to persuasion or coercion by recruiting agents of criminal organizations, but also under the direct guidance of parents or other family mentors.

A diverse body of research positions Juárez as a unique geographical space in which the establishment of this industry has brought about singular processes. The maquiladora industry generated an economic dynamization by attracting foreign capital, which led to the creation of jobs and certain infrastructure; however, it also encouraged new migratory flows, giving rise to new transient populations that have settled into precarious situations marked by pronounced spacial and social polarization, with highly visibilized profound social contrasts (Álvarez). Another sicario describes his thinking process in considering a criminal career path:

> I was not born to be in a maquila. Life isn't easy – whatever I do, I don't see myself applying for credit in a Coppel [Mexican department store chain] store or paying off installment loans in a Famsa [Mexican retail appliance chain] shop. (Alberto)

Modernity, in principle, situates the individual in an environment of growth and transformation, with a promise of adventure, joy, and power, but at the same time there is always a risk of witnessing the destruction of practically everything (Berman 15). Marshall Berman attributes value to modernity in the form of a spiral that breaks apart, that disequilibrates, and leads to disintegration. Modernity as a "unity in disunity" can also be perceived as a "vital experience" that mutates, as nothing stays in place, and "all that is solid melts in the air" (15).

In a similar sense, Valenzuela, in *El futuro ya fue: socioantropología de l@s jóvenes en la modernidad,* which also focuses in on modernity, proposes the idea of the future as something that already was, something intangible and out of reach, that should be understood from a perspective that recognizes uncertainty in all the cultural processes that young people today must experience. Today's youth live the present with great intensity. To them the future is opaque: they know they don't possess the future, most especially the future of opportunities. According to Valenzuela, "for them the future is now, the future already happened" (30).

Another sicario recalls his immediate satisfaction in being able to contribute to his family's wellbeing through his labor in the narcotics industry:

> *I always turned my paycheck over to my mom, although I always did it in secret because my dad didn't want her to have it. I remember the first time: I was still really young and I brought home two thousand dollars for doing two jobs in a row, when the bloodbath here was just beginning.* (Raúl)

The perceived economic benefits to which the sicarios interviewed in this study might aspire represent the strongest reason for them to put their lives at risk as paid assassins. They do know that their lives are essentially disposable, but the pay legitimates the danger and the nearly inexorable end; in this way, they assume the disposition of agnosticism, an unwillingness to look beyond the present moment. The future occupies a space and time that the sicarios of this study don't often contemplate—as if it didn't exist for them. It seems that the ideas put forward by Marshall Berman 40 years ago materialize in the lives of the young protagonists of this study, whose relationship with modernity is one that allows them to be happy but only by assuming a fragility that locates them among modernity's most vulnerable adherents.

The notion of youth takes on a particular social weight in this context in which young people make what might be interpreted as an adult decision to assume a nihilistic life trajectory—not as a phase of self-exploration but as what may be an irreversible and terminal path. Bourdieu explained a while back that youth is nothing more than a word (167); the debate then was not about the simplification of the category of inquiry, but rather how it could be manipulated on a semantic level. Youth is not a given notion, but rather a construct, and because of that, time and place are of utmost relevance. But this premise also implies that youth's most precious patrimony: its present and most especially its future, is also open to manipulation, given the intangibility of the latter term. In other words, the notion of youth tends to conjure up ideas of promise and futurity that cannot be defined; what is most disturbing about young people who become sicarios is that they appear to renounce this promise of youth, perhaps implying that they do not buy into modern society's construct of youth, and should therefore not be considered youth at all. As Valenzuela Arce puts it, "The emptiness of youth illustrates the depth and social weight to which its social construction gives rise" (*El futuro* 30).

However, it would be an oversimplification to assess that the sicarios of this study deny any notion of futurity. Another describes his experience as a sicario as part of a trajectory that remains forward looking:

> *I wanna get out of here and start a family; I wanna get married and have two daughters; I want to study electrical engineering. I don't know what to think – I don't believe I'm going to heaven. I don't feel an urge for revenge – the two times I got mine, I got that out of my system. What I really feel is remorse. I killed my grandfather – it was a stray bullet and it killed the father of my step-father.* (Jesús)

Jesús assesses that redemption is not possible, but his aspirations remain.

Time is actually an element that is implicitly present in the emotions, sentiments, and longings of those interviewed here. While they may evade facing some plausible or even likely consequences of their decisions, they do not shatter any contact with the future. The idea of what they wish for is located primarily in the future; nonetheless, the past torments them and any notions of the future are uncertain, as if it may not be theirs to live. It seems to be a case of a debt that time cannot resolve.

Jesús continues:

> *I don't believe I'm going to heaven. I'm good, but I derailed for a while. I was the best kid, but in junior high I went bad. Here young people go bad, they're disastrous […] Young people really are intelligent, but they get lazy and fall into drug trafficking, and do all kinds of things.*

Youth itself seems to intervene in the lives of young people like Jesús, who "get lazy," perhaps a consequence of immaturity, and make bad decisions that may have irrevocable consequences. Jesús is permanently damaged: he "went bad" and will not go to heaven; but deep down he is "good," and hopes he can get his life back on track. Still, it is not totally clear to what extent Jesús views his going bad, his exclusion from heaven, as an impediment to his mundane desires for an honorable, well-paying career and happy family.

The promise of the future has become the "social breathing" proposed by Michel Maffesoli: the myth of progress for many young people remains out of reach (56). His view traces a longitudinal route from modernity to postmodernity, in which the quest for personal conquests leads to failure in and abandonment of school. In this vein, structural violence remains a key concept for understanding Mexican history; the ideas of development or advancement remain unreal when viewed in relation to outstanding needs in education, health, political participation, and even the functioning of the nuclear family. Youth, in Maffesoli's terms, conforms to "postmodern neocommunities of students," tribes linked by dropping out, feeling excluded, and scholastic failure (56). The dropout scenario draws attention to a broader range of interwoven social, institutional, and personal relations. Failure in school, flight, ought to be thought of as a reality constructed through the school system and in relation to students, but without sidelining other relevant elements, including the political environment, economic factors, family relations, etc.

Modernizing Juárez

"Again, all men will walk straight, all women will smile, all children will laugh. The gates of hell have closed forever," proclaimed the Reverend Billy Sunday on January 16, 1920, celebrating the "funeral" of the consumption of alcohol in the United States (quoted in Manjón Cabeza 41). A circumstance that produced invisible—at least for a while—consequences in Juárez was the implementation of the prohibition of the sale and consumption of alcohol in the United States: the attempt to halt consumption instead fueled an industry along Mexico's northern border, which led to associations that soon diversified their operations and gradually evolved into drug cartels, which along the way stimulated a new market for the consumption of marijuana and opium.

Mexico and Ciudad Juárez saw the arrival of transnational collaboration via rapid growth in the manufacturing sector in the 1970s as an opportunity to pursue strategies of economic development and urbanization. As indicated in the previous chapter, the establishment of a vast industrial complex at the border, the foundation of a new economic order, fueled mass migration from elsewhere in the country. This rapid growth in the midst of poor urban planning has been a major factor in the dissolution or dysfunction of nuclear families, a blow whose social effects continue to be seen decades later. Foreign capital produced an industrial dynamism, but at the same time gave rise to an intermittent floating population of diverse origins and with no roots or support networks in the city, setting the stage for a climate of social and spatial polarization that has unleashed pauperization and violence. Luis Méndez explains the links between the concept of territory, the maquiladora industry, and border violence as part of an indissoluble relationship between land and territoriality (37). The idea of progress here remains in doubt. And the implications for youth born into urban expansion, economic migration, and unrootedness have been significant.

Bauman has outlined how some groups have become superfluous, living "wasted lives"; he calls these populations that have emerged from modernity, suffering its side effects both economically and socially, pariahs. The more modern a society is, the greater the number of its people that are excluded from its basic social networks. "Liquid modernity is a civilization of excess, redundancy, waste, and waste disposal" (*Does Ethics* 180). That is to say, that modernization seems to bring about modernity in such a way that those involved in its advancement end up putting the wellbeing and very lives of others or even themselves at risk, as can be seen in contemporary levels of violence and criminality, and human displacement.

As an addendum to the earlier trends of asymmetry across Mexico's history, it is important not to lose sight of the rise of the internet as a component of everyday life, and perhaps the mass media form that has had the greatest social impact. Its rapid penetration into multiple social sectors has produced a range of what might be deemed side effects of globalization. The internet in recent years makes it possible for youth to lead parallel lives beyond those they live at home or in school, in which what has changed is not the desire to belong, but rather the feeling and forms of belonging (Winocur 576). It is through the internet, more specifically social media, that youth have discovered ways of living and feeling part of something, in tandem with the world in which they move materially. The internet should be seen as a cultural artifact that is also a tool that provides real moments of connection and tangible occurrences (Hine 43). In this way, weak support structures (school, family etc.) may cede influence to purveyors of cultural value systems that have not been conceived with the aim of educating young people to seek sites of belonging from among those authorized by the state or prevailing social norms.

This second modernity is what Ulrich Beck sees as the origin of great risks for many in the world, most especially those living in less wealthy nations, societies where uncertainty regarding long term welfare is a given (9). Likewise, Anthony Giddens has sustained that the world in which we live is dangerous and frightening, signaling that the road to modernity has turned out to be full of potholes, and the loss of faith in progress is a factor that dissolves the narrative of history (55).

OTHERNESS: WORK AS A FORM OF SUBSISTENCE

In Mexico, the use of the term "ninis" became well known when the chancellor of the national university (Univerdidad Autónoma de México – el UNAM), José Narro Robles, claimed that it was a shameful problem that 7.5 million Mexican youth were not working (*La Jornada* 8/13/2010: https://www.jornada.com.mx/2010/08/13/politica/011n3pol). Nini—"ni estudia ni trabaja" (neither studies nor works)—has sometimes been translated to English as NEET (not in employment, education or training). A year later the then governor of Chihuahua, César Horacio Duarte Jáquez (who has been accused of corruption in Mexico and is currently in the US fighting extradition to Mexico to face charges), announced an initiative to recruit so called ninis into permanent paid military service (*Animal   Político   3/28/2011:   https://www.animalpolitico. com/2011/03/propuesta-de-servicio-militar-obligatorio-para-ninis-ya-es-formal/). In Mexico in 2014, the Organization for Economic Cooperation and Development (OECD) revealed that two of every ten young people between ages 15 and 29 neither study nor work. Nonetheless, the most alarming datum is that these young people were wasting an average of 3.3 years of their lives in this situation, a full year greater than the average in other countries surveyed by the OECD. At present, there are no reliably accurate data on how many young people fall in this category, nor of what activities they take up afterwards, but this image of unproductive Mexican youth has been widely accepted.

In addition to the sicarios, Arturo Chacón had the opportunity to interview a young woman who had been convicted as a juvenile of kidnapping and was sent to a reformatory. She admitted to watching over people who had been kidnapped, taking part in roughly a dozen events for which she was paid about $350 each.

> At a party I talked with a friend who invited me to accompany him to work. That's when I realized he was a kidnapper. He told me I'd start off on probationary status and I couldn't say no since he'd shown me everything, including a kidnap victim. The money caught my attention: for every kidnapping that I took care of and turned out OK, they'd pay me seven thousand pesos. It would be once every month or two. Whenever I'd just start running out of money from one, I'd be working on the next one. (Lucy)

The sicarios and other participants in criminal acts related to drug trafficking come from a variety of family backgrounds, but generally speaking they describe their lives were pretty ordinary until around junior high, when upon entering adolescence, without finding the answers they were seeking at the time, they'd drop out of school to start making money in pursuit of material assets that might denote power and prestige, such as firearms, vehicles or clothes, but above all of a sense of belonging to something, accompanied by a sentiment of independence, a means of emancipation from their families or, on some occasions, a way of becoming providers for their families. These young people go through the process that Robert Castel calls disaffiliation, where they feel like they don't belong and as a result are willing to take on high risk activities, putting their lives into a state of latent danger (260). Their decision implies a multifactor justification that goes beyond that of mere financial need; it implies a lack, a hollow space within their subjectivity (245).

> *When I was working in the safehouse, one time I invited my brother to work with us, and then he began kidnapping, too. Once before that they wanted to kill him and my mother took him to Chihuahua. Then the one who wanted to kill him got killed and so my brother came back to Juárez. I worked in about a dozen kidnappings. I just took care of them and fed them, but I could never see them because they were hooded; I wasn't even able to chat with them.* (Lucy)

It might be interpreted that Lucy's labor, which involved some interaction with those who actually performed the kidnappings, consisted mainly of situations in which her responsibility was deeply gendered as one of "care." Those who carried out violent or physically threatening acts of kidnapping, torture or murder were almost always men; her role was to keep victims alive, giving them food and water. Yet this labor of care was deeply dehumanizing as the victims remained socially isolated from Lucy. If she was motivated to join the cartel out of a sense of belonging, she did not really achieve that in her day to day labor. Perhaps a sense of alienation is in part what motivated her to bring in her brother, despite the greater risks his own labor would entail.

The Interamerican Commission on Human Rights (CIDH in Spanish) estimated in 2015 that 30,000 boys and girls were doing a range of jobs for criminal groups—a figure quite distant from that put forth in 2019 by Alfonso Durazo, the secretary of public security in Mexico of 460,000, a difference of over 1500% (Red por los Derechos...). These figures are hard to pin down; how can we calculate the number of minors or youth involved in organized crime? The number is perhaps as liquid as Bauman's metaphor. The industry, with the rises, falls and reconfigurations of its different rival groups, is volatile, ever shifting, and labor within that context is difficult to dimension.

POPULAR HEROES

The growing predominance of labor markets that some scholars have referred to as paralegal, have given rise to new forms of social production (Reguillo, *Culturas*). The fact that participants in these markets call their leaders "bosses" and their organizations "businesses" or "family" invites reflection on the dynamics of organized crime and its public image. The constant cultural production depicting drug trafficking evokes and even glorifies illicit activities as forms not of survival but of progress, belonging and power (Becerra Romero). The frequent news reports on these themes share additional data that can be used by young people who are frequently recruited by these groups.

The gradual visibilization of Mexican drug trafficking organizations over the course of the past century has also given rise to a popular imaginary revolving around the iconic figure of the narcotraficante, with its variations such as the buchón (see Chap. 4), the capo (kingpin), and the sicario. Over the past four decades or so, and with notably greater intensity in the last two, culture industries have turned significant attention to the drug trafficking underworld; film, television, and news media have told stories whose colorful protagonists have captured the public imagination. Likewise, the literary field has seen the popularity of genres of both fiction and nonfiction centered on drug trafficking scenarios. Narcoculture is not just about cultural production, but also refers to a way of life that has been widely disseminated, and sometimes glorified, in which the ostentatious display of wealth among a class of protagonists and antagonists that would normally have no access to elite consumer culture can be especially attractive to young people of a similar class background.

Latin America's acclaimed media theorist Jesús Martín Barbero acknowledges that notions of good and evil become complicated with the narco genre when someone, regardless of their affiliation, saves a victim and becomes a hero. The drug trafficker, relatable to many for his (or her) humble origins, to the extent that representations emphasize good deeds of some kind, often in the paradigm of the social bandit, has become a well-known national (and borderlands) archetype, a figure that may be feared or revered, and admired, taken as a role model.

Music has been perhaps the most notable site of cultivation and diffusion of narco-culture among youth, including narcorridos, which have sometimes gained an edgy image and popularity due to attempts at censorship—the concept of "corridos prohibidos." The recent rise of "movimiento alterado," which has incorporated more explicit images of drug consumption and violence, has exercised notable influence (see studies by Valenziela, *Jefe de jefes*; Montoya Arias and Fernández Velásquez; Ramírez Pimienta, *Cantar a los narcos*).

Dreams and Reality

On the other hand, larger than life tales of excitement, riches, sex, power, and status stand alongside stories of terror, violence, privation, and abuse. The story of an adolescent sicario told by journalist Hérika Martínez reveals the abuses he suffered. He tells of being brought into the group not through promises of money, belonging, and prestige, but rather under threats of violence to his loved ones. The indignities and abuses, both psychological and physical, that he endured are a riveting part of his narrative (*Norte Digital* 11/2/ 2014: https://nortedigital.mx/la-desgarradora-historia-de-un-nino-sicario/).

A 2015 report by the International Commission on Human Rights titled "Violence, Children and Organized Crime" asserts that "various groups dedicated to criminal activities and organized crime operate and use deceit, threats, pressure, and violence to recruit children and adolescents" (62). Moreover, young people "enter the group with little prospect of being able to leave it, which places their personal integrity and rights constantly at risk, leaving them prey to extreme vulnerability" (62–63).

While many teenagers may join up voluntarily, attracted by access to money and independence, and others may be coerced, some may also seek out a sense of belonging to compensate for broken families or lack of parental attention. However, in such a brutal business, it may be hard to conjure up long time loyalty and institutional stability, especially when recruits are so young and vulnerable.

The business, I'm telling you, is bad, very bad. Everything has gotten complicated. And for us, men of confidence are the key elements, and there aren't any guys like this anymore. There's a shitload of assholes trying to become someone in this job, some of them very energetic, but few of them have balls. In the end they all bend. This is endless – it's going to continue, but it keeps getting more complicated for everyone. (Alberto)

Many decisions that were key to getting the protagonists of this book involved in the drug trade were made when they were teenagers, when they were very young, perhaps as a way of refuting the nature of their age. That is to say, they are youth who elect to quickly assume a range of characteristics that are associated with adulthood. These youth modify the spaces of their social world, and within their own subjectivities, they create alternative ways to seek out answers to their problems and fill voids that the world in which they grew up left empty. Their everyday experiences and tasks make up their present, their reality (Valenzuela, *El futuro ya fue*).

The current scenario for some sectors of the youth population is the link in a chain that endures with the force of a locomotive that keeps running through the years without losing potency. Alonso Salazar mentions at the end of *No nacimos pa' semilla* that a situation cannot be controlled that is not looking to be controlled to begin with, and even less so when those that give meaning to the lives of those involved remain ingrained in their ways of socializing, within scenarios of violence as opposed to progress, when the common denominator of death is a fundamental reference.

Nonetheless, some young people seem to find stability in organized crime. As Alberto asserts:

> *I like my job because it's what I know how to do. If I went about doing something else, I don't know what it would be. I've been in this for ten years and I've fought through it all.* (Alberto)

We might comment here while none of the sicarios were actively working at the time of their interviews, Alberto is the only one that we know of who went back to organized crime, returning to killing in 2013 soon after his final interview with Chacón, and remained active as a sicario through at least 2016. Since then Chacón has not heard anything from or about him.

Becoming a Man

Youth is often theorized as a period of transition from childhood to adulthood (Echari Cánovas and Pérez Amador), which makes it a social category that lends itself to ambiguity, especially in areas such as criminal justice in which determinations need to be made regarding whether to treat an offender as a minor or an adult. Sicarios, who are regularly recruited from among this age group, as noted above, think in the same ambiguous terms as they mete out organizational justice on behalf of their employers. They may treat sons and daughters of targets, some of whom may fall in their own age group, as innocent children, while they kill teenage members of rival trafficking syndicates without remorse. In this case, age is not the determining factor of transition from childhood to adulthood, or from youthful innocence to grownup responsibility. Other factors determine when this line is crossed.

So that's the difference [...], a novice doesn't even know how to shoot a pistol. What I was saying was it was that novice's first time, the first time he went chasing after someone, and when he pulled the trigger of the long gun, from the banana clip, he ended up grazing everybody who was with us. I mean he was hitting the people who were with us. He didn't know how to aim, or to shoot. I mean it would be better not to arm a novice for that reason, because he could end up killing the rest of us. (Anastasio)

Experts on youth recognize that this category is a social construct applied differently across cultures, social classes, demographic sectors, history. Moreover, it is usually thought of as a transitional process, in which young people gradually assume characteristics of maturity and adulthood (Dávila León 86–87). A life cycle defined by the very crude set of concepts of "education, activity, retirement" would locate youth at the tail end of the first, transitioning into the second. The novice described by Anastasio above, in this scheme, is still a child because even though he's working for the narcos, he's still very clearly in a learning phase.

Anastasio clarifies:

You need to get them in sight, aim, and on the first blast, the first shot, hit them right where you want to. I mean, I've realized that the people who are professionals, you can tell who they are, because from a distance they are going to make hits where they aim, and they don't need more bullets – the target is going to die, simply, with one bullet. Sometimes there are guys who fire a lot of shots or they use up a lot of bullets trying to hit the person. But there's one, and you could see this on the body, that had just one bullet wound, and they said that was because the assassin was a professional, because he shot only once, because he's been taught, trained to not waste even one bullet.

The transition implied here from novice to professional is parallel to that of a student graduating from high school or college and entering the labor force. In this scheme for interpreting the category of youth, there are of course many other aspects that might determine whether a young person is understood to be fully an adult, including their ability to support themselves, their assumption of family responsibilities, among others. What is clear in Anastasio's assessments of his fellow sicarios is that although making the transition in terms of professional knowledge and autonomy itself does not necessarily imply an unambiguous move into adulthood, the transition might happen at any age.

Anastasio recalls a more ambiguous case (here we recall and extend a passage quoted earlier in this chapter):

> *In my cell, the youngest was thirteen years old. This thirteen year old minor was a sicario. He was addicted to killing people – that kid loved killing people, and, well, right now he's locked up awaiting trial. That kid, as far as what I knew, well, yeah, he killed like ten people [...]. He was one of the professionals, he was well liked, the boss's favorite. At his young age, he was a professional.*

Anastasio's comments about this "minor," a professional assassin with ten presumably well executed murders under his belt, locate this young sicario in a gray area. He was clearly not one of the "innocent children" who would be spared on a job, yet, barely a teenager, he remains a "kid," recalling the case of "The Hollywood Kid," a young mara salvatrucha chronicled by Óscar and Juan José Martínez, who started killing at age 12, and racked up over 50 murders over the course of his career as a sicario.

However, Anastasio makes clear that the transition to adulthood for a sicario is not gradual or protracted:

> *So, from fifteen on up, fourteen on up, you're no longer a child [...]. Well, there aren't any children, I mean there are young people, but young people don't go around doing this, you know. But, yeah, from like fourteen on up, not anymore.*

The 13 year old is still a kid, but by 14, not anymore.

Tony clarifies further, pointing out:

> *young people, thirteen, fourteen, fifteen years old, already with the banana clip, assaulting, killing people just because "I'll give you five hundred pesos to go and kill that guy for me" [...]. They were recruiting children, or well, young people – for me the fourteen, fifteen year olds are children – to kill people. I saw it happen. Live through it first hand – no. Because, well, the people I was with, well, they were already, you know, they already knew what they were doing. Some no, no, they were still kids when they were eighteen. But there were people who had always been in this business since, well, they don't know what else to do.*

While Tony had not himself worked directly with young adolescents, he knew about them, and had to imagine what the recruitment of "children" to the sicariato implied, especially as some of his own sicario peers were "still kids" at 18.

Tony lays out a two pronged moral assessment of the situation. He is troubled about the recruitment of teenagers, who are still children, and affirms that some of them are still just kids throughout their teens, even if they are working as assassins. But he also sees some of his young colleagues as adults because of their awareness of their actions, their competence to assume responsibility for their actions. Like Anastasio, he seems to see a transition to adulthood occur with many teen sicarios, who start out as kids, but as they gain professional expertise in their line of work and come to understand the full moral and social impact of their trade, can at another moment be held accountable for their deeds. Yet Tony contends that not all those who are targeted for murder have reached this state. The excerpt above actually begins with a lament:

> There were a lot, a lot of innocent people, a lot of innocent people who we should not have lost, especially young people, thirteen, fourteen, fifteen years old, already with the banana clip. (Tony)

The fact that they had been recruited, and were themselves killing – a banana clip is a curved magazine common on automatic weapons – and therefore being targeted and, in many cases, murdered, does not itself imply that they were old enough to be held responsible and to be effectively assigned a death penalty by their organization's enemies. Tony, who at other moments is defensive of his participation in the drug business, claiming that the organization gave him the ability to help his family and others in need, many of them young men who had been abused or abandoned by their families, here is critical of his organization's treatment of some of these same young men, who are exposed to danger from a very young age, many of them dying while still "innocent."

CONCLUSIONS

Just as researchers, legislators and judges, as well as ordinary people grapple, with defining the difference between youthful innocence and adult maturity, sicarios have difficulty articulating the nuanced differences between youth and adulthood. They employ terminology implying maturity or immaturity (children, professionals) in their descriptions of their work environment, referring to both their colleagues (those recruited to become sicarios, and who take on this job and identity), and those who they are assigned to pursue. It is important for some of them not to kill "innocent children," a term they use to refer to young bystanders, those not directly involved in the narco business, even as they recognize that their own ranks incorporate many minors, who at least initially are seen as "kids." At first these kids may be "novices" who barely know what they are doing, let alone how to do it, but within a very short period they may become "professionals" whose awareness of the damage they do, the pain they cause, implies an assumption of moral responsibility. They undergo a form of education that includes learning skills (how to use weapons, how to plan an assault) and also gaining a deep understanding of the repercussions of their work.

Tony is aware of "a statistic that there were more deaths here in Juárez than in Afghanistan, the war in Afghanistan," which he knows translates into "death" and "suffering." Youth, among sicarios, is short. The transition to adulthood may be more a practical imperative than a natural process of psychological, social, or cognitive maturing, coming of age, and it may not happen in the protracted way it is experienced in other sectors. It is not unusual nowadays for youth to be prolonged, with young people continuing to live with parents and putting off taking full financial responsibility for their lives or starting their own family until well into their twenties or thirties. Sicarios, in contrast, are confronted with life and death situations in which potential killers and victims may be legally under age, but may already be de facto adults.

CHAPTER 4

Sicario Masculinities: Feeling Reckless and Afraid

THE SENTIMENTS OF SICARIOS

They're good people, they conduct themselves nicely, they are not disrespectful. Obviously they impress you with the SUVs they drive. What attracts me? What impresses me? At first, their clothing, that they dress well, the colognes they use, the watches they wear; that is, yes, appearances impress me [...]. Then obviously their telephones, what phone model they have, if it's one of the latest ones, or their SUVs. (Rosina)

Narcoculture represents and promotes a culture of hypermasculinity and of unambiguously defined and distinct gender roles. And within narcoculture, the role of paid assassins is perhaps the most extreme manifestation of this masculine hyperbole. While occasional figures, whether real or fictitious (or some combination thereof), of female drug kingpins (La Reina del Pacífico, la Reina del Sur) or killers (Camelia la Texana) have captured the popular imagination, a major component of the fascination they provoke is their exceptionality (Ramírez Pimienta). The vast majority of people who make their living as employees of criminal drug syndicates, most especially those whose trade is that of sicario, are men, and the vast majority of those men are imagined and portrayed with very conventional masculine attributes. Nonetheless, seen from up close, their relationship to hegemonic notions of masculinity may be more nuanced.

Sicarios, following Sayak Valencia, are men for whom violence as a component of labor serves as "an implement of personal self-affirmation and, at the same time, a means of subsistence" (91). The sicario trade is a very male phenomenon, as it responds to "the fear of emasculation that hangs over many men in the face of the precarization of labor and their consequent inability to raise themselves up in a legitimate way in the role of male provider" (90–91). For Valencia, this is a new form of male violence that is endemic to, and indeed is a defining characteristic of, the contemporary context of "gore capitalism," which no longer repudiates violence as a criminal act, but rather creates "another sort of socialization" and assigns it "another status: that of respectability" (71). This chapter looks at this brutality with a focus on how it plays out in notions of masculinity, including both how men who routinely commit acts of severe violence see themselves, and how some others who know them intimately see them. In order to understand the lived experiences of narcomasculinities as expressed by sicarios (and their female admirers), this chapter looks to the structures of feelings that motivate different actions by sicarios and other actors within the context of criminal drug syndicates.

A Woman's Views on Narcomasculinities

Aside from the occasional female capo or the perhaps more common female dealer or smuggler, the female archetype most associated with narcoculture is that of the buchona. A buchona is, according to urbandictionary.com "a strikingly good looking woman who tends to be the girlfriend/ love interest of a gangster." This archetype frequently appears in music videos and soap operas dressed in clothes that reveal a curvy figure, heavy makeup, and flashy jewelry. Buchonas are generally assumed not to be directly involved in the criminal activities of the men they accompany, but rather are attracted to the lifestyle their relationships with men involved in the drug trade make possible for them. Just as these men are often portrayed through stereotypes of extreme machismo, buchonas conform to narrow stereotypes of women as sexual objects who draw on their ability to physically attract men—powerful men on whom they are ultimately dependent—for their wellbeing or advancement in life.

> *I started working in a bar when I turned eighteen. I was a cocktail waitress and I liked to party, so it wasn't difficult for me. The work is easy; you just have to serve and make conversation [...] – I learned quickly. In the cantina, you*

meet them before long [...], you spot them right away, by their tips, the music they play – you immediately realize which side they're on or who they're with. Always expensive bottles, the most expensive, blue ticket, the expensive Buchanons, Moët. They've left as much as a thousand pesos for a tip, and that's a lot. (Rosina)

Parallel to the archetype of the buchona is that of the buchón: "those whose distinguish themselves through grandiose manifestations or exaltations in dress, consumption (cars, motorcycles, yachts, houses), arrogance, easy spending of money, and belief that success is obtained through violence" (Alvarado Vázquez 138), a male archetype prominent in narcoculture to which many sicarios may seek to conform.

While the ostentatious consumption of prestige goods might contribute to the image of a range of masculinities, it is especially notable and deep rooted in the context of narcoculture. As José Manuel Valenzuela Arce noted in 2002, "It is not enough to possess the items, it is important to make them visible, conspicuous, as this is the way to redeem and to justify the risks" (*Jefe* 154). Moreover, in narcoculture, questions of ethics regarding means to personal enrichment are overridden by a value system based on traditional notions of masculine power: "With the boundaries between good and evil shattered, the roles of police and thieves are blurred. The lifestyle associated with the power of drug trafficking casts off the morals that functioned when the dimensions of consumption were linked to the ways of obtaining them" (13). According to Valenzuela, in the context of narcoculture, "machismo can [...] be seen in the ostentation of consumption" (176–77); indeed, displays of opulence are one of its major defining characteristics.

Shaylih Muehlman, in her ethnographic study of borderlands narcoculture, observes the social signification of wearing alligator boots: "more than a stylistic reference, it reflects the economic dynamics in northern rural Mexico by portraying the tough cowboy and survival of rural adversity" (70). Her research focuses on men from impoverished and marginalized circumstances who engage in criminal drug trade for economic, but also clearly sentimental reasons. In a notable case study, her interviewee describes "how working in the trade as a low level narco made him feel and how it allowed him to see himself" (82). Specifically, "it made him feel brave and powerful, and it made him feel like he was providing for his family" (82), all clearly feelings of male realization. However, the cultural context she observes is not one that values self-fulfillment; it is not enough to feel manly and secure, but rather it is essential to be seen by others as manly, tough, and successful. Muehlman adds, "And, of course, it made him feel attractive" (82).

The buchona, then, is a woman who shares the value system of the macho men of Mexican drug trafficking culture. Indeed a buchona's attraction to a buchón may enhance the latter's status and power. And while for men, narcotrafficking may offer a means to power and social status confirmed through conspicuous consumption, for some women an easy route to social capital may be through their mere attachment to socially powerful men, in the role of "trophies." In the context of narco-corridos, site of perhaps the most widely diffused and influential images of narcoculture, women are most often portrayed in strictly traditional roles, and one of those is that of the woman as "commercial trophy" constructed in such a way that "it is not even necessary to seek her out, rather she comes on her own, attracted by money and power" (Valenzuela Arce 165).

> *I've been hanging out with these people for five years, and I don't regret it. They're good people, they've always treated me well and inspired my affection [...] The best of my life was spent with [a former narco boyfriend]. I learned a lot from him; I did many things, went to lots of parties, travelled, and never lacked for anything. Actually, [...] I travelled more with him than with my family.* (Rosina)

Rosina takes advantage of her ability to conform to the archetype of the buchona, the trophy girlfriend, buying fully into the value system of con-spicuous consumption, and amply enjoying the comfort and security afforded by the lifestyle offered by her narco romantic partners. Her par-ticipation does not reflect a mere shallow materialism, rather is based on deeper feelings. In her case, this involves a profound affection and sympa-thy for her narco beaus.

> *Later you start to get to know them and it changes completely [...] Their lives, for example, they've told me things – there are those whose parents have died and have siblings, and this was their only option to find work. The majority of the guys with whom I've spoken are from Altavista, Bellavista, almost all from that sector [...] and I've visited these places and they are very humble. I've also met guys who got out of jail and no one else was willing to hire them.* (Rosina)

While the masculinity that men involved in public drug syndicates publicly display may coincide with the narrowest stereotypes of Mexican machismo, the women who get to know them intimately may observe and appreciate attributes that would seem to contradict popular conceptions of what has been called narcomasculinity (Biron), a contemporary hypermasculinity that coincides in many ways with traditional and hegemonic masculinities in Mexico.

The garish displays of power and wealth, and the implicitly brutal means by which they are obtained—the qualities that draw women to them, contrast starkly with the humility, respectfulness and tenderness that seduce women more deeply, prompting them to fall in love. Many men who elect to participate in criminal drug organizations come from circumstances of extreme economic precarity, and the feelings of male vigor that access to large quantities of cash may produce in them, may only superficially mask deeper feelings of vulnerability that can perhaps not easily be shed. Indeed, the power of men involved in the drug trade is never secure, as the violence of this milieu leaves them open to the constant threat of incarceration or assassination.

Power and Vulnerability

A provocative study on the masculinities experienced by "halcones" [falcons], the name used for the usually teenaged lookouts that support drug traffickers, in Tamaulipas, argues that the construct of the powerful narco contrasts deeply with his everyday reality: "The same place where stories are told of money, power and women, incidents fill the barrio with blood, the traces of fights, gunshots, of burnt up cars, of flames burning all over the place. It's where they collect the cadavers of life long pals" (Córdova Plaza and Hernández Sánchez 566). Halcones learn that "every narco masculinity is made up of nerves, and above all fear, a great deal of fear" (567). Moreover, boys growing up in narco controlled barrios learn that fear is fundamental to their marginalized lives, whether they themselves become narcos or not. However, they learn that fear is a necessity to maximize one's own alertness in situations of physical danger, may also learn to channel it—that is, that "it can be substituted with other emotions, such as fury, rancor and hatred" (567).

Tony, the sicario cited at length in Chapter I reflects on his experience in killing:

In the beginning, it was like a … rush of adrenaline, but at this point the truth is that, yes, the fear of whether I will come home or not … you start thinking about what my family will do without me. Well, they are things you start thinking more about [...]. Fear is what warns you in any situation; if you say you're not afraid, that's a lie.

The substitution of emotions (adrenaline for fear, fear for fury) indicates both the intensity of the everyday lives of sicarios, as well as the deep seated contradictions that may underlie their sense of masculinity. The dividing line between fear, an emotion that may signal an impulse to cower or retreat, and hatred, an emotion that may fuel violent action is unstable. Tony adds, "Fear ... if you don't have fear, you don't know hatred."

The Case of Anastasio

We were working for an ex-military man, and he's the one who gave my brother and me orders. Since we were the most daring ones, he'd send us. He'd give us the address and tell us exactly what the person we were going to pick up looked like. We'd go in the SUV, with the driver, and we'd wait for the individual to leave. Then we'd stop them in the middle of the highway. We'd use our arms to make them get out, we'd get them out of their car and into the SUV. Our job would be to take them to the safe house and then we'd leave them there. (Anastasio)

The best known representation of traditional Mexican masculinity is Octavio Paz's collection of essays *The Labyrinth of Solitude*, whose second chapter, "Mexican Masks" describes Mexican men as stoic individuals, who are conditioned to never reveal their feelings or otherwise demonstrate vulnerability: "the ideal of 'manliness' consists in never 'cracking'" (Paz 29–30). The Spanish expression "rajarse" means to crack, to open up, to give in, to back down. It implies cowardice and weakness, but also candidness and sentimentality. As one sicario put it, "you turned into another person, completely heartless, because you were going to take another person's life, I mean you can't involve your feelings" (Ulíses).

To be clear, according to Paz, in this seminal 1950 essay, Mexican men were not in a position to live up to the ideals of manliness that they displayed. Their relationship to this hegemonic masculinity implied dissimulating: dissimulating cowardice, simulating impotency, dissimulating debility, dissimulating passiveness (40–43). Masculinity needed to be performed ("mimicked," according to Paz: 44) following conventions that justified men's superior position in their relationships with women, and upheld social institutions and hierarchies.

In a later chapter in the same book, "Sons of la Malinche," Paz further develops his theory on the dynamics of Mexican masculinity and gender relations through an exploration of the verb "chingar," which might be translated roughly as "to fuck" or "to fuck over." Writes Paz, "For the Mexican, life is a possibility of fucking or being fucked. That is to say of humiliating, punishing and offending. Or the inverse" (Paz 78). This orthodoxy of Mexican masculinity implies a violence in social relations, in which masculinity is asserted through acts of dominance and displays of power exercised over women and other men.

The authority of criminal drug syndicates, built upon violence and the threat of violence, as well as the ostentation of material affluence, appears to offer a path to achieving the status of "el gran chingón," the ideal of Mexican machismo (Paz 81). Salmo recalled his life as a successful sicario: "my brother, may he rest in peace, and I now were the most fearsome guys in the neighborhood." They asserted their prowess "charoleando," a metaphoric expression that implies brandishing a dazzlingly impressive credential. By being members of the dominant syndicate, they assumed its aura of power and authority.

As Tony, put it, "It was the money, and the partying, making yourself known. I mean … you believe you're Superman […], you own the world." Masculine prowess was asserted both through territorial control realized through publicly visible—sometimes sensationally so—violent acts, and also through publicly visible affirmations of this dominance seen in the flaunting of luxury goods.

Clearly, Rosina, the woman quoted above, was fascinated with this aura of power and authority. It impressed her and drew her in, even as she sensed and eventually experienced danger. She worked as a bartender, and it was in the bar where she would frequently wait on customers involved in drug trafficking organizations, some of whom she would go on to date. However, just as her lifestyle, which some might identify with the archetype of the "buchona," implied the thrills of luxury and extravagance, it also implied tangible danger. According to Rosina:

Sometimes at my job, they'd murder a cocktail waitress. And while the bullets would be fired in her direction, there would be stray shots, and they are marked in the walls.

She adds:

At the beginning [...] maybe I'd think nothing would ever happen to me because I had yet to witness any ugly situations. But after I did, all kinds of things would go through my mind.

This was a world not only of exaggerated masculine privilege but of extreme male violence. The sicario that killed the enemy would become, at that moment, el gran chingón. But in this violent world, he might also take blows at any time. Of the five narcos that Rosina discusses having dated, she knew two to be dead. Furthermore, sicarios, those who carry out the most absolute assertions of male authority—by killing those that their organization wishes to subordinate, nonetheless occupy a subordinate position themselves within the organization that employs them. They are expected to obey orders, and if they don't do precisely what they are told, they may face violent consequences.

Anastasio repeatedly articulates his role of obedience: "we had to do what the boss ordered"; "we took orders from the boss who was in charge of the market." He explains:

The order they gave us was to not kill innocents. We didn't kill women or children, unless the woman was the target, only then, because we didn't kill women and children who had nothing to do with our assignment. If they were the wife or son of the victim, we respected their lives – they had to be respected. And when someone was sloppy, I mean if they shot down the family, they would be in trouble. They used a club, made of hard oak wood, and they'd take us and beat us. They'd actually torture us for making mistakes. They'd torture us and lock us up in a punishment cell.

Anastasio makes clear here that while the acts of violence he committed may have conferred on him an aura of power, he was never the owner of those acts, and his actual power was always subordinate to that of the superior authority who gave the order to kill. Any killing in excess of orders received did not bestow any meaningful feelings of empowerment, but rather called into play a violent reinforcement of the limits of the sicario's status within the hierarchies of male domination of the organization. As Pierre Bourdieu notes, "Manliness, it can be seen, is an eminently relational notion, constructed in front of and for other men" (53). In this case, the power acquired by Anastasio upon killing the enemy is embedded in a larger set of male power relations in which his role requires strict obedience, and keeps him subordinated to superior men whose authority is unchallengeable and who wield absolute power over him.

This is then a dynamic of male on male violence, realized within a context of male hierarchies of power. While, as Rosina notes, women involved with these men and with these organizations might occasionally themselves be targeted, or be placed in danger due to their frequent proximity to the violent context in which drug trafficking organizations operate, the acts of violence are part of an all-male social system in which women, for the most part, do not directly figure. In fact, the mere presence of women might sometimes suppress the eruptions of male on male violence that might erupt at any time, as Rosina explains, below.

GENDER AND VIOLENCE IN JUÁREZ

For example, sometimes there were big parties, and there were a lot of drugs, pistols, lots of women. Actually I enjoy drinking, but beyond that I haven't done anything else. That's what I don't like. Because, I don't know, probably with so many people in one place, other people might show up and make total chaos. Or among themselves there might be hostility, or a woman [...] But actually when they are with a woman, or when they are with several women within their circle, they try to drink less [...] You might say that they do take care of us. (Rosina)

Julia Monárrez writes, "The murders of more than 200 women in Ciudad Juárez since 1993, and the torture and rape of almost 100 of them, are painful testimony to the vulnerability of girls and women on the border and to the male violence perpetrated against them" (153). The context that Monárrez describes, that of the patterns of feminicide that emerged in Ciudad Juárez in the 1990s, seems at odds with that described by Rosina of habitually violent men holding back their impulses when (certain) women are around. While violence is prevalent in Rosina's world, and she is acutely aware that women may be victims of that violence (regarding the murder of waitresses, she avows: "there were several in that bar"), she repeatedly describes the men with affiliations to drug trafficking syndicates that she dates as respectful and caring with women—they are "good people."

Likewise, in the previous quote Anastasio insists that at least some sicarios—he speaks from the context of those working under a particular boss—were not only forbidden from killing "innocents," but were subject to harsh physical punishment for killing anyone but those specifically identified by the syndicate as a target. And these targets were not the kinds of victims of feminicide described by Monárrez and other scholars of that phenomenon, which Valenzuela Arce defines as "the maximum expression of misogyny" (*Sed* 52): poor women, often migrants, working in maquiladoras or other low paying jobs. Rather, according to Anastasio, "almost always those who we were killing were kidnappers, extortionists, rapists."

In fact, Anastasio describes part of the mandate of the sicarios in his group to serve as foot soldiers in "the war […] against the pigs." The pigs, "los marranos": "are the people who killed children, women, everything that you cannot do." Tony, likewise, insists that: "I tell you I can't, definitively I tell you I can't – not children, not women." While these declarations by no means imply that drug trafficking syndicates are likely to be benevolent organizations that serve society by protecting women and children, it appears that there are contexts within them in which, even among sicarios, the lives of women and children are held in higher regard than those of men, and the rules governing violence may assume a very different gender politics from that underlying Juárez's notorious feminicides.

Of course, the fact that the role of sicario is nearly exclusively male serves to reinforce the differentiation of men and women into distinct, and narrowly traditional, roles, in which men are providers and protectors and women are caregivers and objects of male sexual desire. Exceptions (reputed female assassins such as Joselyn Alejandra Niño, "La Flaca"; Valeria Coronado Hernández, "La Wera Sobacos Pantera") generate sensational press coverage, but are very few in number. Drug syndicates are without a doubt profoundly traditional as patriarchal institutions. However, it is interesting to note the shift that occurs in the image of Ciudad Juárez between the publication in 2000 of Julia Monárrez's seminal article "La cultura de feminicidio en Ciudad Juárez, 1993-1999" and the discussions of the surge in drug related violence in Ciudad Juárez occurring around the year 2010, the first shown to be an alarming and apparently endemic structural violence directed by men toward women, while the latter, although rarely discussed in gendered terms, is, in the vast majority of cases (over 96% of murders in 2009, according to Cruz Sierra and Cervera Gómez 122), male on male violence: "what in principle we might call masculinicide" (Cruz Sierra and Cervera Gómez 115).

While we must take issue with the casual use of this latter term, narcos do not go after random men, nor do they murder men for being men, the shift in balance from decade to decade is remarkable. And the statistics for Mexico, as a country, are notable. According to a study by the United Nations Office on Drugs and Crime, the global average percentage of homicide victims that are men was roughly 79% in 2012, whereas, in

Mexico, the proportion was nearly 90%. Notably, this rate is not significantly different from that of other Latin American countries known for drug trafficking, such as Colombia, El Salvador, or Honduras, but stands in sharp contrast to figures around 80% for such countries as the United States, Peru, Bolivia, and Chile. Of all those countries mentioned above with homicide rates above 20 per 100,000 population, only the US did not vary from global averages regarding gender of homicide victims (https://www.unodc.org/gsh/en/data.html).

MALE LIFE, BARE LIFE

Returning to Anastasio's recollections, cited above, it would seem that among at least one subgroup of sicarios of Juárez, some human life has value, while some doesn't. Without assuming that the code of conduct he cites was by any means universal (we might consider, for example, the notorious LeBaron family massacre of November 2019, in which all of the victims were women and children), for Anastasio, the attention to not killing women and children coincides with the chivalrous treatment that Rosina describes receiving from the narcos she dated. But the killing of men is endemic to the culture of criminal drug trafficking syndicates in Mexico, whose commercial successes are gained not by superior product or catchier marketing campaigns, but by physical conquest of marketplaces. That conquest is frequently achieved by killing rivals, who happen to be, in their vast majority, men. Furthermore, those men are presumed to be criminals, whose life means little to the state infrastructures of criminal justice, which are unlikely to devote significant resources to pursuing the murders of men assumed to have been themselves dangerous criminals. From the perspective of many, society is better off with more dead narcos. Social outrage materializes only when the victims of narcoviolence fall outside the ranks of the criminal organizations, when women, children or certain classes of men assumed not to be involved in the drug trade die—that is, when there are so called innocent victims, as was the case with the 2010 San Fernando massacre of 72 migrants, or the Villas de Salvárcar, in which, as indicated in our introduction, the assassins mistakenly targeted young students not involved in drug trafficking. But the murder of addicts, dealers, lookouts, smugglers, kidnappers, extortionists, assassins means very little. And this idea of criminal male lives devoid of value is absorbed within the culture of narcotrafficking organizations itself.

So the boss who was in charge of the market [...] would order us – because he didn't like what people were doing, like the extortions – you know, like, that was not our way, and he didn't like them to be doing that. And if they saw them doing something, they would figure out who it was, and send us to kill them [...] Yeah, so it was something that, well, they didn't like to see happening in the city. That's why a group of us was cleaning up all of Juárez, getting rid of all the filth. Even today they still say there's a lot of filth, a lot of pigs. It started many years ago, you know, when the slaughter began here, that they would say that he was the pig butcher, Licenciado Pig Butcher. (Anastasio)

Hermann Herlinghaus's contemplation of what he understands as the "violence without guilt" within Mexican narcoculture might be explained to some degree by this ethical stance that rationalizes violence among narcos. This "ethics without morality" that Herlinghaus links to an ideal of "unbound stoicism" (53) is no doubt troubling and difficult for Anastasio himself to assume, as might be inferred from the short amount of time he spent working as a sicario, as will be made clear below.

While it may not be true that criminal drug syndicates have been uniformly careful about not harming innocents (e.g., a 2019 case in Juárez involves the killing of a five year old at a kindergarten graduation event)—indeed, these organizations are generally known for causing all kinds of harm beyond the realm of those directly involved in narcotics sales, smuggling and related criminal activities, the assimilation of the devaluation of the humanity of the male criminal expressed here is striking, especially when considering that it is not just members of rival groups who may constitute this category of what Anastasio refers to as human "filth"; to many juareneses, who were often not made aware of the group to which a given set of assassins or victims belonged, all narcos were narcos, all sicarios were sicarios. There is no public interpretation of the Juárez violence of this period that attributes to any element of it the moral integrity and righteousness expressed here by Anastasio:

Yeah, yeah, cleansing, getting rid of everything that is no good, the real pigs, the ones who enjoy killing children, yeah. I mean, think about it, if it was one of us receiving orders to kill someone: "I want you to go and kill so and so; he'll come out of his house in a car of whatever color, and will come out at such a time," and you had to be there waiting for him. And if his car came out, and if he was there, with his wife and children, you got him out and you killed only him on the ground. You didn't go shooting at the car because there were people, innocent people, in there. If we went after him, only him, we'd stop the car, get him out, on the ground, and as for the rest of them, his family, we wouldn't do anything.

To be clear, Anastasio as a sicario had no say in who he was sent to kill. If there was, as he claims, a kind of code of honor within his unit that ensured that only those deserving to be killed, those whose life had no value, would be targeted for assassination, this was likely the idiosyncrasy of the individual giving those orders. Portraying the mission of this unit as one of cleaning up the city of human filth was no doubt a way of motivating sicarios to carry out their assignments with enthusiasm, and without guilt.

Likewise, sicarios developed their own strategies for justifying their acts. Tony emphasizes that the financial gains achieved through his work have not gone toward mere frivolous purchases of materialist ostentation; he's actually been able to offer palpable help to people that has made a difference in their day to day lives:

> *The truth is I don't regret what I've done because like good and evil, I've known good people, people who also have suffered since they were born, through their youth, and I've been able, as much as I can, to help them in whatever, in giving some care or some support, like a brother or even like a father. And while I don't regret what I've done, I do regret the harm I've done to my parents. But like I'm telling you I met some good people, I've known very good people that nobody would think were involved in this. It would be to help people in need, only that, because there are people who need help because they're hungry, in need, for money, you know, a house.*

In direct contradiction with the dehumanizing posture articulated by Anastasio in his reference to some other narcos as "pigs," Tony goes so far as to criticize people for not recognizing the humanity of those involved in drug trafficking:

> *When they say that organized crime is just death, in reality they're not seeing beyond the violence that harms people, that speaks badly of people, and all that. They don't see the good side, how they help the community, how they help friends who are in jail, right?*

This contradiction is a prominent undercurrent running throughout the testimonial narratives of sicarios, who do not, in the end, represent "figure[s] of an ethics without morality" (Herlinghaus 53), at least in their own self configurations, but rather a conflictive morality that pits their own humanity—which they cling to even as they routinely commit heinous acts—against that of those men, many of whose biographical profiles are very similar to their own, whom they kill with utter stoicism. Their victims are the enemy of their organizations, and the scourge of society, yet they are their peers.

Anastasio found an early justification for killing in feelings of revenge:

> When I started to be driven more from rage, more from anger, was when they killed my cousin and my uncle [...]. I had an uncle who was a drug trafficker, right? My cousin and my uncle got targeted by a group of men, and they shot them down, and me and my brother were there, and we managed to run away. I mean, well, they were looking for us because in fact me and my brother ran off, and they went around asking where we'd gone. Yeah, after that every time that I did something, that I killed someone, I did it for the revenge of our family.

However, while Anasatasio and Tony had to come to terms with their actions on an individual level, the organization itself provided an infrastructure that would instill in them motivations and justifications to kill. And this infrastructure was without any doubt fiercely heteropatriarchal in nature.

PRODUCING NARCOMASCULINITIES

Guillermo Núñez Noriega and Claudia Esthela Espinoza Cid argue that "narcotrafficking (and therefore narcoculture) is a mechanism of sex-gender power that produces sexuality and gender in its subjects: ideas, values, attitudes, perceptions, practices, relations, subjectivities, sexual and gender identities, organized, of course, in accordance with heteronormative and androcentric parameters" (93). There are several intersecting assemblages of influence at work here. Aside from the hegemonic values associated with masculinity more generally in contemporary Mexico, most especially in the precarious social contexts of Ciudad Juárez from which sicarios most often emerge, there are a range of widely disseminated—at least since the 1970s—notions of narcomasculinities that circulate through popular media (narcocorridos, telenovelas, etc.), and finally there is the localized culture, what might be thought of as a corporate culture, that is enforced within the specific criminal syndicates in question. Whether or not cartels really "exist" in the way most people understand them (Zavala), Anastasio and other sicarios refer to belonging to a specific cartel to whose culture and values they must conform.

Núñez Noriega and Espiniza Cid posit that criminal drug trafficking syndicates interpellate young men through their cultures of masculinity, and the means they offer to attaining male prestige: "The possibility of recruitment, in other words, of reproduction of the criminal organizational structure, can be better understood through these cultures of gender that constitute the caldron of cultivation for the production of subjects yearning for manhood, anguished about their sex-gender precarity, open to learning, and anxious to pass the test of 'true' manhood" (110). Anastasio describes his process of becoming a sicario:

> So, when I got out of the CERESO, [...] I mean in the CERESO is when I started to meet a lot more people [...] because there in the CERESO it's all gangs, the gangs of the Juárez cartel, the Sinaloa cartel, you know, they keep them separated there, and since I worked for the Sinaloa cartel, they had me in the Sinaloa cartel section, and I started meeting more and more people there. And when you're inside, they call the CERESO, they call it a school. We called it a school because you learn more there than you would on the outside, you learn more on the inside. And when I started to meet more people there, they start telling you, "look, when you get out, we can give you some work." You do this and that, right? And, yeah, when I got out, well, I started getting involved.

The all-male space of the prison was an ideal place for networking and male bonding. Anastasio adds:

> When I got out of the CERESO I already belonged to the gang that's on the inside, I mean, [...] like they say, I was now one of their brothers.

If in general the personnel of a Mexican criminal drug trafficking organization is itself overwhelmingly male, the sicario line is very nearly exclusively so. The sicario's is a job whose defining task, murder with a firearm, is deeply associated with masculinity, especially in Mexico, where, as Paz asserts, life is defined by two possibilities: *chingar o ser chingado*. It is the job that undoubtedly generates the most fear in both its targets and in its perpetrators, but that also gives the latter the greatest opportunity at feeling (and flaunting) a heightened sense of virility. Anastasio describes his first assignment as a sicario:

> That's when [my brother and I] became, yeah, sicarios, taking the life of a lot of people. Well, the first time, yeah, is ugly, you know? it's ugly [...] Yes, you're gonna feel ugly, you feel ugly, right? Because you're taking a person's life, and

you don't know if that person has children, if he has a mother, but in that situation it's you or him. And the truth of the matter is that, you know, like they say, you need to summon your courage, your macho.

This virility that helps Anastasio go through with the morally reprehensible act of taking a human life becomes entwined in his day to day work as a sicario, especially as he establishes his standing among sicarios. Núñez Noriega and Espinoza Cid signal that it is this reliance upon and achievement of virility through violence, not just economic factors, that fuels participation in criminal drug trafficking syndicates: "drug trafficking promises its participants or those aspiring to participate (through a variety of incentives and attractions) the expectation of fulfilling a project of gender identity" (120).

But, as Anastasio notes repeatedly, "it is ugly"—indeed, he uses that same word four times when describing his feelings upon undertaking his first assassination (above), and four more times when explaining why he killed only four people during his stint as a sicario:

I was just getting started, but, I mean, to my shame, you know, they might say "huh! so few!" But they were only a few. It's something that is ugly, that is ugly. I don't have any reason to say I got twenty or thirty or fifty, and that's why I'm going to feel big, I mean, I'm going to be full of myself. Looking at it now, yes, it is ugly, yes it is ugly.

He describes feelings of ugliness, which coincide with the fulfillment of the promise of an enhanced virility. His inability to come to terms with these feelings may be what led him to abandon this career path after a relatively short time in this job. However, he also recognizes what drew him to it, the sentiments that motivated him to participate. He dwells on the ugliness, but more animatedly refers to feelings of exhilaration. He may have killed only four victims, but those were some exciting moments for him. He first gets a sense of these latter feelings upon witnessing a particularly brutal assassination.

GORE MASCULINITIES

I was there and they grabbed somebody, a rival, and they cut off his head while he was still alive. They nabbed him and cut it off, they cut off his head and they cut him into pieces. Well, that hit me hard, you know? It leaves you stunned and, well, I got hit with adrenaline, I got hit with adrenaline [...] Yeah, yeah, so the adrenaline got to me, like It got me more excited. (Anastasio)

Sayak Valencia presents a compelling argument regarding the options for men from marginal backgrounds who wish to conform to basic requisites of heteronormative masculinity, such as being a reliable provider for their families. I would argue that for many years, certainly from the 1970s until the early years of the first decade of the 2000s, an additional option for many Mexican men was migration. While migration to the United States, as migration scholars have shown, may have provoked revised attitudes regarding gender norms, and revised gender roles, at least in contexts of heteronormatively defined families, migration to the US, for many men and for many years, offered an more likely alternative route to fulfilling societal expectations for men, most especially that of being a dependable breadwinner. Recent scholarship in gender and migration studies has made this case (see Broughton). However, since the rise of the border industrial complex and the deportation regime (see Dear, De Genova and Puetz), it has been harder to migrate, and harder to avoid being repatriated. Certainly since 2007, the easiest option for many Mexican men wishing to achieve some version of their ideals of virility through money, sexual prowess, and, most importantly, power over other means, has been the hyperviolent realm of criminal drug trafficking syndicates.

Recalling the murders of his cousin and uncle, which Anastasio used to justify his own acts of extreme violence, he relates:

> *Yeah, now every time I did something, I mean killed somebody, I did it for the revenge of our family. I mean, well, it was an exchange of bullets, right? And. well, you just throw yourself into it, like in a movie [...]. You're afraid and it gives you adrenaline, I mean, it's up to you to hold it back or bring it down [...]. So you're there and this guy wants to run, and when he starts running, then pum! pum! pum! pum! pum! He wanted to run and so he didn't get the chance, he could no longer be given a chance. And in reality you don't know if he's going to run or if he'll turn it around and hit you from behind, and so anybody could win. He was running and you're right with him, now with our gun drawn. And so I got one of them and shot: pum! pum! pum! pum! pum! pum! pum! and so he went down.*

Valencia posits that the "endriago," a monstrous, dragon-like incarnation of contemporary Mexican masculinity (89), has emerged as a major archetype of narcoculture, and indeed of contemporary capitalism. She argues that one of contemporary capitalism's most extreme but not most uncommon manifestations, which she calls "gore capitalism," has become increasingly brutal as some of those in pursuit of its bounties have increasingly turned not only to the exploitation of laborers, but to "the most explicit violence as an implement of necroempowerment" (15), the latter term implying a will to power that displays an utter disregard for human life. The endriago, as one who enacts "processes that transform contexts of vulnerability and/or subalternity into possibilities of action and selfempowerment" (205-6n1), exemplifies this axis of violence.

And with a predisposition to commit outrageously bloody and grisly acts—for money—the endriago would seem to be best exemplified by the sicario. While Anastasio, along with the other sicarios interviewed here, presents a somewhat more nuanced and circumspect image, the unbridled emotion expressed by Anastasio in shooting down the enemy in the above passage (fear that he transforms into an adrenaline rush, in line with experiences described by fellow sicario Tony earlier in this chapter) would seem to confirm Valencia's suggestions. While Anastasio might not be a monster, he could use his ideas of virility to summon the courage to turn into a monster.

Adrenaline is another keyword, appearing four times in his testimony: three times when recalling his witnessing of a beheading and quartering of a body by another sicario, and one more time, above, to introduce his only detailed description of one of his own murders, a word echoed in the onomatopoeia of the pum pum pums that perform the shots of his gun, 12 in all, punctuating his story with enhanced exhilaration. He describes the rush of adrenaline emerging from feelings of fear ("You're afraid and it gives you adrenaline"), recalling the reflections of fellow sicario Tony, cited earlier in this chapter, suggesting that the dividing line between the powerful killer chingón and the meek and frightened chingado is precarious. The stoicism that expresses valor inevitably masks feminizing fear.

Anastasio does give some information about his second assassination, which was actually not carried out with a gun:

> *The second assassination was, it was by hand, without any weapon or anything, by beating. I pounced on the head of this person, and I jumped and jumped and jumped on his head until…*

Valencia struggles to understand the human motivations behind the cruel and brutal killings carried out by drug trafficking organizations, which often incorporate publicly visible displays of carnage. She finds answers in the kind of violent and ruthless, indeed excessive, masculinity described by Paz in *El laberinto de la soledad*, but in a grisly and exaggerated form. These are murders characterized by what has been called overkill: severed limbs, publicly displayed mutilations, obvious evidence of torture (see Fox and Levin). While the violence that Valencia considers, and indeed the brutality described here by Anastasio, are monstrous, Valencia's largely theoretical approximation misses the nuance of lived experience. Anastasio becomes a monster—perhaps because it gave him a generous biweekly paycheck (he says he was paid "eighteen thousand pesos" or close to a thousand dollars every two weeks), perhaps because he was terribly shaken by the murders of his relatives, perhaps because he was lured into ever more violent behaviors while living while in prison among men with violent histories, perhaps because he was drawn in emotionally by the potential for an adrenaline rush—his monstrousness materializes only occasionally in his testimonial narrative about his life as a sicario. He describes what he feels after committing a murder in this way:

> *Well, you feel desperate, nervous, startled, like, you think that they're going to come, and they're going to do the same to you, that they saw where you went to hide.*

Anastasio's murders may have sometimes been gory, but it seems reductive to view him as a mere pawn to gore capitalism. He falls into the life of a sicario, and enjoys it to some degree, but does not seem able to accommodate himself into it. And he leaves after only a few killings. It seems that while adrenaline is key to inspiring his most brutal acts, fear is a much more decisive emotion in his story.

Reckless Masculinity in the Face of Fear

Like Anastasio, Tony makes reference to the "adrenaline" he feels at the moment of a murder. Salvador Cruz Sierra has argued that much narcoviolence is generated from the "joy of a reckless masculinity" ("Violencia social" 293). He argues that "adrenaline, excitement, hormones imply a body that feels relations to aggression, death, sex, violence," but notes that "fear is a threat to masculinity, at least the hegemonic variety" ("Violencia y jóvenes" 628). It is interesting to note that of the sicarios interviewed, the one who has the most to say about the emotional thrills provoked unleashed by committing acts of violence, is also the one who most dwells on his fears. And his rushes of adrenaline and fear seem to be deeply intertwined; it is worth repeating a passage from Chacón's interview with Tony, quoted earlier in this chapter, here:

> *At first it was like … adrenaline, but at this point, yes, the fear of: will I return or not return home? You start to think, what will my family do without me? but, yeah, they're things that you start to think more about. Fear, if you don't feel fear, you don't know hatred. Fear is what warns you about any situation. If you say you feel no fear, that's a lie.*

Tony's reflections here are worth comparing to those of Anastasio, who initially presents himself as reckless and fearless in a description of the murder of a kidnap victim that he witnessed prior to himself becoming a sicario:

> *So, when I saw him dead in his truck, dead, where they killed him, I felt no fear. I approached where he was to see him because I always, ever since I was little, I was a person who likes to be in the middle or right in the face of problems, or fights […]. And even nowadays when something happens, I haven't lost that. I want to be there, get right in front to see exactly how it is, how it turned out.*

Cruz Sierra describes the emotional charge felt by those exercising narco-violence: "Violence can be accompanied by toughness, coldness and affective disconnection, but also satisfaction in one's capacity of domination," noting that any potential fears are often quelled by drugs ("Violencia y jóvenes" 629).

However, the effects of drugs are temporary, while the fears provoked by a life deeply embedded in violence are profound and constant. Anastasio recognizes that violent acts provoke a simultaneous rush of adrenaline and fear. As he put it earlier, "You're afraid and it gives you adrenaline." For Anastasio fear is fundamental to his experience as an assassin:

> *It's the same fear that you feel, the same fear that you feel, because yes there is fear, yes there is fear. Whether you killed him or you didn't kill him, there's fear that there will be retaliation anyway, that they'll follow us, you know, and the problem will get bigger. And that really brings you down.*

It is perhaps astonishing that Anastasio not only admits his fears, but that he describes them so emphatically. Here he repeats himself twice, word for word, in his expressions of fear, repeating the word "fear" five times, leaving no doubt that these feelings have powerfully marked his memory.

If he sounds reckless, or "sadistic," to use another term suggested by Cruz Sierra to describe narcoviolence ("Violencia social" 298), when he describes his adrenaline rushes, this "reckless masculinity" is only fleeting. It's something he may have summoned, felt, and displayed on some occasions, but it does not seem to capture the larger composition of his psychological profile. Anastasio's masculinity is multifaceted. It reflects an ability to commit unbridled violence, but it is also nuanced by both fear and a persistent sense of morality, constant self-judgment.

Rosina signals that the reckless masculinities of narcoculture are seductive:

I like that they don't think about the future, and don't pay attention to what they spend. They live in the moment and that's it; they don't end up owing anything, they have no regrets, and they feel no fear.

However, she is also aware that living recklessly is inspired in a fatalism that is ultimately a means of coping with a deadly sense of fear:

It's clear to me that I won't be able to be like this my whole life, but I like not thinking about what will happen later. I'm living the way I want to, without regrets. Nobody can be sure about how they'll be living a few years from now, or even if they will be living. [...]. That's something that [my narco lovers] taught me, and if they never said it, with their deaths I learnt it: it's better to live and that's it.

Rosina not only lost two hypermasculine and reckless narco lovers, but also was witness to the assassination of another "buchona," an event that also deeply affected her:

I'd like to leave all of this because I'm tired of the operatives and the executions. I hope my life will change, but I've had bad luck: I've already lost two partners who were killed and what can I do? That time in the Fronterizo bar, I didn't know her, but I saw her die, and I am scared that one day, for no reason, it will happen to me.

Reckless and Afraid

Fear and exhilaration are the emotions that the sicarios interviewed most often express when referring to the scenes of violence in which they are protagonists. Their recklessness, stoicism in the face of danger, and thrill at the power implied in annihilating the enemy contrast starkly with the anxiety and feelings of terror and dread that haunt their everyday lives as a direct consequence of these same moments of violent abandon. Their lives thus take on a bipolar element that might seem difficult to reconcile, and ultimately drives some of them to step aside. As far as we know, only one of the sicarios interviewed returned to the business; the others all had resolved to seek other employment and life trajectories.

Alberto, the interviewee whose career as a sicario was reactivated in 2013, expressed dismay at the state of the sicariato: "for us, men of confidence are the key elements, and there aren't guys like this anymore." He expressed frustration upon observing that many sicarios are "energetic, but few of them have balls; they all bend." They are unable to turn off the fear. Adrenaline generates energy, but they cannot maintain feelings of fearlessness; their courage is not intrinsic, but ephemeral. He doesn't elaborate on what he means when he says they "bend," but he would likely look with some contempt on the other sicarios interviewed here, all of whom withdrew voluntarily from the cartels, and many of whom speak frankly and often of the fear they'd felt.

The masculinist ideology that forms part of the drive to bring down, to kill, those pegged as rivals allows them to fulfill some requisites of contemporary manhood. They earn money to provide food, shelter, even some luxuries for their families; they gain access to prestige goods (clothes, cars, electronics); they impress and attract some women, including some considered especially desirable and who would otherwise ignore these young men; they obtain reputations that make them feel powerful and important in their neighborhoods and among some of their peers. Yet they end up living under a shadow of dread that their families will be targeted, that they themselves will be murdered, that they will be judged as evil and will be condemned to hell. These latter feelings no doubt threaten their feelings of empowered virility, but they are too overwhelming to ignore. The practices that promised to enhance and consolidate their manhood end up shaking it profoundly. Ultimately the majority of sicarios interviewed seem to have rejected the values underlying the configurations of virility that characterize the context of gore capitalism, and sought other ways of living that deny the possibility of ever attaining the hypermasculinity—which they've found to be a hollow hypermasculinity, an empowerment that engenders an incapacitating fear—to which they had once aspired.

Salvation Amidst Everyday Assassination

There is no doubt that criminal drug trafficking organizations stimulate and exploit traditional antisocial aspects of traditional Mexican masculinity in a culture that is profoundly male and excessively violent. However, it is less clear whether they profoundly or permanently alter the masculinities experienced within their ranks. Indeed, many of those recruited to be sicarios are very young, and while many may die young, those that survive, like Anastasio, Tony, or Salmo, may move on, seeking out other lifestyles that ultimately give them less access to feelings of power, but allow them to feel better about themselves, even if this implies a loss of masculine prestige, as they seek justification for their violent acts, admit their fears, or turn to God for forgiveness. In other words, these ex-sicarios make clear that they do not possess inherent or learned characteristics that mark them for life as criminal sociopaths; rather they are men who make horrific choices that may later come to weigh on their conscience, and motivate them to seek ways out, even if it means losing the ability to display symbols of male prestige, social capital that they ultimately feel to have come at a moral cost.

Tony confesses, "yes, I believe in God, and I turn to him, I pray to him, every night." And Salmo reveals, "I'm now seeking the ways of God." Indeed Salmo feels at peace because:

All the harm we did, for me, what I did, my God has already forgiven me, yes, he's forgiven me for everything.

CHAPTER 5

Fury as a Tool of Evil

LOCATING THE ROOT OF EVIL

I remember that they asked me to kill him and since he was tied up, well, it was easy, I just aimed and fired at him. What I remember more, because it made me feel bad, was when I cut off a guy's head. It was the first time. I turned yellow and I think my pressure dropped because I got really weak, like I was about to pass out. (Alex)

The scenario of violence and terror in present day Mexico emanates from a context of organized criminal groups, popularly known as drug cartels, whose territories they are reputed to control, as if they were unsanctioned nation states. For many, including especially those who, like the residents of Ciudad Juárez in the years 2008–12, have seen the sometimes spectacularized violence of the cartels up close, drug trafficking syndicates are the purest manifestation of evil that they know. Certainly, the highly visible mass produced violence on display there in those years, with public and mediatized exhibitions of blood, torture, mutilation and dismemberment, suggested a highly dehumanizing set of practices that might seem inexplicable by any logic not rooted in evil.

For those whose knowledge of the narcoviolence of Ciudad Juárez in those years is second hand, a glance at the book *Dying for Truth: Undercover Inside the Mexican Drug War*, published by the authors of El Blog del Narco, startles the senses by presenting an up close look at the everyday

© The Author(s), under exclusive license to Springer Nature Switzerland AG 2022
A. Chacón Castañón, R. M. Irwin, *Listening to Sicarios*, New Directions in Latino American Cultures,
https://doi.org/10.1007/978-3-030-94118-5_5

gore of the period. El Blog del Narco itself, an online forum that is active to this day (for more detailed critical information, see Eiss), has become an authoritative source for up to the minute information on Mexican drug trafficking violence and other news. The information it imparts is often startling for its graphic representations of cruelty. It was founded March 2, 2010, by an individual who claims to have been interested in how drug traffickers make a living by killing, kidnapping, mutilating, and selling narcotics. Its main sources have been people from the narcotrafficking community itself, which gives it credibility: "The idea of creating Blog del Narco came about when the communication media and government tried to make it look like nothing was going on in Mexico, due to the fact that the media are threatened and the government apparently bought out" (https://elblogdelnarco.com/acerca/); the blog lets people from all over know the details of the disputes among the cartels, told from within. Its anonymous contributors reveal details regarding the clashes among drug trafficking organizations that could not be covered by identifiable reporters or news media for fear of repercussions from the cartels. The above mentioned book is a chronicle of a year of narcoviolence in Mexico, laying out minutiae of specific acts of violence, identifying the organizations and sometimes the individuals involved, whether as perpetrators or victims of violent acts. Most shocking, however, are the visual representations: an onslaught of blood and gore seen in page after page of crime scene photos. For those who can stomach leafing through this book, or browsing the more spectacular entries of its website, it is difficult to interpret the carnage as anything but an apocalyptic manifestation of evil.

The cartels, with their colorful capos, Joaquín "El Chapo" Guzmán; Amado Carrillo Fuentes—better known as "El Señor de los Cielos" [Lord of the Heavens]; Miguel Ángel Félix Gallardo, "El Padrino" [The Godfather] or "El Jefe de Jefes" [Boss of Bosses]; Sandra Ávila Beltrán, "The Queen of the Pacific"; Edgar Valdez Villarreal, "La Barbie," for many represent evil at an organizational level, a manifestation of the violences of the capitalist free market system taken to the extreme—what Sayak Valencia has called "gore capitalism." And certainly the celebrity kingpins, who may earn upwards of hundreds of millions of dollars a year, can be construed as the personification of the violences wrought by capitalist greed as they order and strategize extortions, kidnappings, hits, and warlike incursions onto rival turf. Nonetheless, these figures sometimes assume mythical characteristics, whether through their often heroic depictions in narcocorridos, or through media representations of their rags to riches success stories, abilities to outsmart and thwart law enforcement agents, and powers over state authorities. If the capos are evil, it is an evil that inspires awe, an evil that draws comparisons to that exhibited by powerful entrepreneurs, politicians or other figures of great influence who had to fight their way to the top (see Valenzuela Arce, *Jefe de jefes*).

Often it is the criminal syndicates themselves that seem to more concretely embody evil. The Zetas, known as a group of highly trained Mexican army deserters that first gained fame as the enforcement arm of the Gulf Cartel, later became an independent rival organization involved in the narcotics trade, but also, most notably, sex trafficking, arms trade, extortion and kidnapping. The Zetas gained worldwide notoriety in 2010 when 72 bodies of undocumented migrants were discovered in San Fernando, Tamaulipas. The victims were reportedly massacred for being unable to respond to extortion demands and refusing to collaborate with the Zetas (Pérez Aguirre). Less than a year later, another 193 bodies were discovered in eight mass graves in San Fernando, their murder again attributed to the Zetas. This group, which built a reputation for brutality by staging visually spectacular murders and publicly displaying mutilated cadavers, for many exemplifies the core evil of Mexican drug cartels (on the rise of the Zetas as an embodiment of evil, see Grayson and Logan).

Some Mexican scholars have looked specifically at the ways in which young men, recruited as adolescents by drug cartels, are portrayed as inherently different from other young men in contexts of criminal justice through a "punitive distinction between citizen-enemy" (Salazar Gutiérrez 28), a construct that implies these youth are not legitimate members of society, but rather dangerous outsiders. From this perspective, the responsibility for the violence that threatens the equilibrium of everyday life in contexts of drug trafficking is assigned to these young "enemies." While some critics do not condone "demonizing certain groups of offenders," others claim a need for "a legislation of struggle, of combat" against mainstream society's antagonists in an imagined war (29), a strain of thinking clearly aligned with the Mexican government's rhetoric of a war on drugs.

A concept that has been applied to process the evil acts carried out by Mexico's drug trafficking organizations, especially in places such as Juárez where they have penetrated deeply into the everyday life of residents from all walks of life, is that of terrorism. Campbell and Hansen interpret this violence as follows: "Narco-terrorism is deliberately planned and choreographed by the leaders of drug cartels or their criminal gang and political associates, not by the rank-and-file cartel or gang members who carry out the densely symbolically laden terroristic actions" (163). Terrorism is a term whose usage has been varied and often imprecise, but is employed most often to refer to personal suffering or damage to an institution or enemy regime by means of an attention getting act of brutality that generates a radical destabilization or crisis: "in contrast to most violence in conventional warfare, the immediate casualties and damage caused are thus not the prime objective of terrorist attacks, which is to inflict psychological pressure on a third party who have become the 'audience' or 'spectator' of the outrage" (Griffin 12). The evil associated with terrorism by this definition does not match up easily with organized crime (see González Rodríguez), whose goals in meting out violence seem targeted more at identifiable victims of enemy camps, including state actors that get in its way, than they do at bringing down the government or radically destabilizing society at large. After all, drug trafficking syndicates remain business operations that depend on some degree of economic and social stability in order to maintain markets for their products. Nonetheless, many who have lived through the surging violence, seen family members and neighbors killed, and been eye witnesses to brutal acts, have felt terrorized by forces that they can attribute only to evil.

Institutionalized Violence

Many Mexicans do not see the drug trafficking organizations as acting alone in bringing this evil to their cities, neighborhoods and doorsteps. Many agree that another contributor to this context in which, following Sergio González Rodríguez, public spaces all over Mexico have been turned into "battlefields," is the Mexican state. Mexico's governing bodies have cultivated not only dysfunctional state institutions that cannot guarantee citizens' basic rights or access to justice, but also state violence: bloody landscapes derived from erratic strategies for opposing organized crime. The statistic of 102,859 first degree homicides registered by the National Institute of Statistics and Geography (INEGI) and the National System of Public Security (SNSP) during the presidency of Felipe Calderón (2006–12) remains a flashpoint for many Mexicans, who see the Calderón presidency as an incubator for the heightened levels of violence that remain endemic in Mexico to this day, indeed a platform for most the violence that occurred at that time in the country, and for the cultivation of the phenomenon that is the focus of this book: "*el sicariato*" or trade of paid assassins. The period that followed, that of Enrique Peña Nieto's presidency (2012–18), effectively experienced an increase to 122,889 murders. Since then Mexico's murder rate has run at over 25 for every 100,000 inhabitants nationally (see AP News 1/20/21: https://apnews.com/article/homicide-coronavirus-pandemic-latin-america-mexico-a90c2a172f39ab2546de465c73a60543), which is higher than that of Colombia and Nicaragua.

It is thus not productive to think about this violence as being outside the state's own constructs, a nuanced view that has a long history: from Max Weber—who considered that violence should be analyzed in function of perpetrators and their intentions, and made clear that it was the state that monopolized violence's legitimate uses, to Walter Benjamin—who contemplated violence as the origin and essence of law.

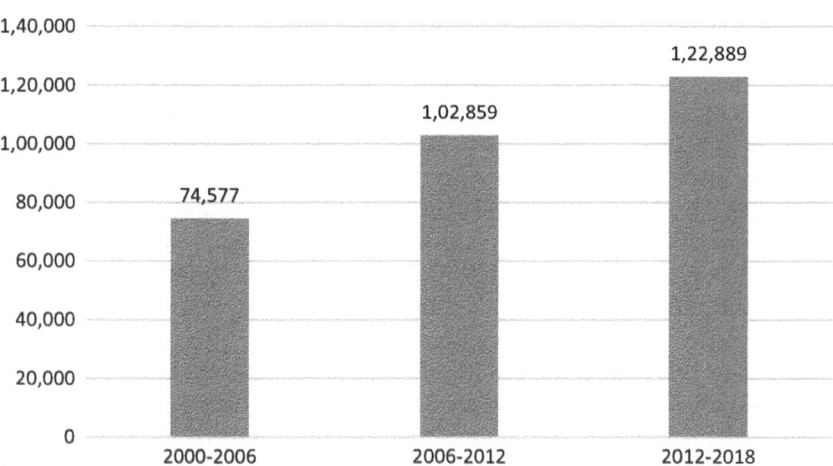

Homicides by Presidential Term

In the only interview of Ismael "el Mayo" Zambada García, friend and associate of Joaquín Guzmán Loera, who was recently convicted of major crimes in New York in a highly mediatized trial, the kingpin, assured Mexican journalist Julio Scherer in 2010 that the war on drugs is a lost cause because "narcos are embedded in society, right along with corruption […] As for the kingpins, jailed, dead or extradited, their replacements are there waiting." Certainly that is what happened with Guzmán, as his criminal conviction had little effect on the Sinaloa cartel, as Zambada simply stepped in to replace him. The landscape laid out by this capo can, at first glance, be read in two ways. The first is that drug trafficking in Mexico might appear to be a dragon with a thousand heads: if one is cut off, it will simply sprout another, and then another, in a cycle that has no end. The second locates drug trafficking as one more aspect of a generalized culture of corruption, as something deeply embedded in Mexican culture, with the obvious implication being a symbiosis between the institutions that seek to combat drug trafficking and the drug cartels themselves. This reading connects very clearly with Zavala's arguments, in our first chapter, that the cartels don't exist. What doesn't exist, more precisely, is a world of evil cartels and good government agencies as two distinct and ethically opposite entities; in fact, there is no way to define a dividing line between the two.

NATIONAL EVIL

The fact that Calderón's war on drugs not only failed to curb but actually incited drug related violence reveals a context in which state intervention has been useless as a control mechanism. It has become difficult to even think of the state as a leading perpetrator of necropolitics—it might be easier for the cartels to bring down the state than vice versa. In this sense, many consider Mexico to be a failed state due to its inability to carry out many of its basic functions and inspire confidence in its populace (see Dear 134–39; Benítz Manaut). And if the vacuum of power left open by a weak state is thought to have been filled by drug trafficking organizations, who impose their own tax systems, control large sectors of commerce, and manipulate law enforcement and judicial sectors, then perhaps Mexico is better defined as a narcostate (Dear 127–34). With the crisis of violence reaching new levels in 2010, some civil organizations of the borderlands made a public request for intervention from the United Nations' Blue Helmets, a proposition that did not go forward as it was rejected by Mexico's federal government, which was forced to assume a defensive posture with regard to its ability to maintain order and security. Whether the state is seen as merely too weak to stamp out evil or as directly complicit in the evil deeds it publicly claims to be combatting and is responsible for containing, the Mexican government, to many, seems to occupy a subordinate position to the drug syndicates (Appel). These ideas of the Mexico as a "failed," "weak" or even "narcostate" have become common. Carlos Fazio in his book *El estado de emergencia* has argued that Mexicans live in a "state of exception" in which criminal groups have broken tacit codes that maintained the symbolic barrier between legal authority and illicit activity, unleashing battles not only among armed criminal groups, but also political and economic elites in a bloody crossfire in which the general public has been witness and victim.

But the day to day violence on the streets is carried out by individuals who are not likely to ever become millionaires or larger than life legends of popular *corridos*, and whose access to power is fleeting and more probably an illusion—and who in many cases may themselves end up dead before having any chance of overcoming their ordinariness or marginality. And yet it is these less extraordinary individuals who carry out the day to day brutalities that become what are for many the most tangible incarnations of evil. It is the paid assassins that bring that evil down to the level of the individual human being: these are the *malandros* and bad hombres that have been batted about among politicians and media outlets, whose public identities are defined by their inherent wickedness, their evil, and yet in their anonymity their most malevolent acts are much less abstract than those of the media star capos, and therefore can more easily be imagined in more human terms. But is it really possible for us to define humans as evil? As Jean Baudrillard sees it, "The idea of evil as a malign force, a maleficent agency, a deliberate perversion of the order of the world, is a deep-rooted superstition" (160).

Theories, Explanations, Excuses

In the book that evolved from his doctoral dissertation, *Mexican Drug Violence*, the esteemed photojournalist Teun Voeten discusses the different meanings that Mexico's narco warfare has communicated from an international perspective. He links Mexico's violence to the cultural baggage of armed conflicts and civil wars in Latin America, depicting a violent panorama in recent decades across the region. In this vein, Juan Carlos Garzón, citing Rubio and Lomborg indicates that "between 73,000 and 90,000 people per year die a violent death by firearms in Latin America, which is three times the world average" (Garzón: 14). This recalls Beck's notion of "societies at risk," in which the struggle is not among social groups but rather huge economic sectors that inherit an integrated globalization, or what in Giddens's understanding of modernity implies a change in social order in which individuals experience a solitude that obliges them to seek substitutes for social bonding. Part of the latter's argument is that there is a dark side of the risks and dangers of first world modernity, which must confront a larger global reality of perennial inequality.

In Latin America in 2014, a regional average of 16.4 of every 100,000 youths were killed in incidents of assault by firearm (Otamendi). Mexico has not been an exception; according to data from 2017: "Nationwide, murder is the principal cause of death among youth and adults between the ages of 15 and 44" (*El Economista* 11/1/2018: https://www.elecon-omista.com.mx/politica/Asesinato-principal-causa-de-muerte-de-jovenes-en-Mexico-20181101-0022.html). In this context, Voeten thus sees this violence not as evil, but rather as an endemic sociocultural phe-nomenon, in some cases the legacy of authoritarian regimes, but also the product of a neoliberal economic model that has generated significant inequities that impact democracy by weakening government institutions.

The literature on *sicarios*, which first emerged from the context of Colombian narcoviolence in the 1980s, has frequently sought out under-lying social causes for the sometimes shockingly brutal acts carried out by these professional killers. Rather than attribute their horrible deeds to an abstract concept of evil, scholars, creative artists, journalists and others have sought to identify the circumstances that allow for the emergence of a social category that on the surface seems utterly diabolical: the serial assassin who is not mentally ill (as might be the case of an independently acting serial killer), but rather is carrying out a peculiar form of labor.

Several theories have come to prevail, including what might be called the "no future" argument based on circumstances of poverty and chronic lack of economic opportunity (exemplified in Víctor Gaviria's 1990 film, *Rodrigo D: No Future*). According to José Manuel Valenzuela Arce, "Poverty and inadequacies associated with poor and deficient diet gener-ate unstable foundations that limit the development of children and youth" (136). Likewise, poor education, unemployment, and generally meager living conditions apply great pressure to young people to seek out solutions "in spheres of informality and paralegality" (137). While some marginalized youth may have the means to look for opportunities else-where, migration—long a viable option for adventurous Mexican young men—has become an increasingly difficult and often perilous option which may pressure more of them to turn to criminal organizations.

Another potential issue underlying Mexico's rise in violence is that of neglect. Scholars have focused in on histories of abuse and abandonment in contexts of family, school and other social institutions in understanding why some young people may turn to careers in crime. Some argue that many "delinquent youth were expelled from their homes or the environment in which they were raised [and] grew up with profound resentment and lack in affection" (Cisneros and Robles 457). Neither family, nor schools, nor church offer sufficient mechanisms of support and guidance to enable many young people to integrate into their communities as responsible citizens.

Another concept that has been explored in the context of Mexican narcoviolence is that of "*gandallismo*," which points to the lure of power and respect that drug trafficking organizations offer, at least at the localized neighborhood level, to those living in precarious circumstances. According to José Lorenzo Encinas: "The reality is that gang members obtain not only wealth and money, but in their barrios of origin they experience a sensation of greatness, social respect, a power based on the fear that they instill in others," a status that allows them to overcome "being the marginalized kids from the hood" (65). The "gandalla socialization," following Encinas, refers to not only the cultivation of a lust for power, but opportunities to obtain immediate satisfaction with minimal investment. Miserable living conditions make for an uncertain future in which the predominant mechanisms of socialization oblige those experiencing these conditions "to take maximum advantage with minimal effort" (Encinas 61), that is, to jump at the chance for easy money, rapid ascensions to social status, and immediate access to power and influence.

There is no doubt that all of these dynamics underlie the personal histories of many if not all *sicarios*. However, if circumstances, society, history, global economics or ineffective government is to be blamed for the individual or collective acts of violence committed by the ranks of paid assassins within Mexico's drug trafficking organizations, can these unprecedented and often gruesome acts of violence be attributed to forces of "evil"? To what degree should those committing these wicked acts, those employed as *sicarios*, be held responsible for them?

Returning to Baudrillard, he distinguishes between two concepts: "Evil is the world as it is and as it has been […] Misfortune is the world as it ought never to have been" (144). This image of underprivileged youth drawn to crime by unfortunate circumstances beyond their control contradicts the popularly held idea that *sicarios* are evil, an abstract concept that is understood to be a pure and inherent social force. The contradiction between classifications of unfortunate—"the wretched of the earth" driven to make decisions and commit acts that are destructive to society and themselves—and evil—spawns of the devil, natural born and incurable evildoers—is significant. "It is misfortune that is most distinctly opposed to evil and to the principle of evil, of which it is the denial" (Baudrillard 145); indeed if adverse circumstances are the root cause of evil acts, then it becomes difficult to pinpoint the source of evil in the activities of *sicarios.*

Agency becomes an important question. Some scholars, in analyzing the contexts that produce narcoviolence, employ a rhetoric that implies a lack of agency on the part of those drawn to drug trafficking organizations, a rhetoric of "sole option," "lone possibility" (Cisneros and Robles 454–55) or "bare life" (Herlinghaus). While evil forces may underlie their acts, *sicarios* themselves are not evil because they lack the resources that would give them the agency to avoid them. This view is in sharp contradiction with that articulated passionately by some other critics: "assassins are assassins" (Héctor Aguilar Camín, quoted in Valenzuela Arce, *El futuro* 163). The latter position implies an utter lack of faith in rehabilitation, redemption.

Banal Evils

Philosopher Hannah Arendt, reporting on the Eichmann trial in Jerusalem in 1961, contemplated the rise of totalitarian regimes as a consequence of the failure of moral conscious and of common sense. An altered state of reality evolves in which violence is assumed to be inevitable, and evil becomes banal. For a soldier, killing is a duty following from orders that must be obeyed. That's just how things are. Later, in her 1969 article "On Violence," she endeavored to articulate the relationship between state hierarchies of power, the institutions that carry out their directives, and violence. From her perspective, anyone can commit the most terrible of acts by simply ceasing to think.

While the context of German Nazism and the genocide carried out during the war emerged from a hegemonic ideology that permeated Germany, the case of organized crime in Mexico is different. There is no ideology that justifies the violence of drug trafficking organizations as ethical; instead, those committing narcoviolence seem most concerned about personal gain in the form of power, prestige, affluence, all of which are unattainable by legal means. What both cases share can be seen in the way those committing acts of extreme violence play down or deny individual responsibility. For Mexican drug cartels, the banality of evil plays out in characterizing targets or victims as rivals who are dispensable and whose elimination is necessary; sicarios are trained and conditioned not to consider the consequences nor the aberrant nature of their acts. They let themselves to get swept along; the assassinations they carry out represent the fulfillment of orders, which allows them to feel that moral responsibility lies elsewhere.

Adriana Cavarero in her book *Horrorismo* looks at the terror evoked by mass violence in contexts such as those of war viewed from the perspective of its victims. She writes "in a time when dead soldiers are a forgotten minority when compared with the percentage of civilian victims" (Caravero 12). The bloodied landscapes charted across the territorial brawls of drug cartels invite reflection along the lines proposed by Caravero.

On the morning of November 6, 2008, a decapitated body was found hanging from a central bridge in Ciudad Juárez. A large cloth, also hung from the bridge, attributed the murder to a criminal syndicate that claimed control of "la plaza," which translates as "marketplace" or "territory," and warned that the death and torture of 23 year old Sergio Arturo Rentaría Robles, the victim of the crime, marked "the beginning" (*El Agora* 11/6/2008:   http://www.elagora.com.mx/Cuelgan-de-puente-a-decapitado,8888.html). Dozens of commuters waiting at daybreak at a nearby bus stop encountered the headless body as if it were a piñata that morning when for several hours police and firefighters endeavored to lower the body that was suspended by a rope. The missing upper extremity was located hours later in the Plaza del Periodista at the base of a monument honoring journalists known as "the paperboy" (a sculpture of a paperboy making deliveries). This latter act took on additional significance for the city when, several days later on November 14, journalist Armando Rodríguez was murdered, receiving ten bullets upon coming out of his house to take his daughters to school (*La Jornada* 11/14/2008: https://www.jornada.com.mx/2008/11/14/index.php?section=politica&article=014n1pol).

The execution of the journalist is a tragically paradigmatic outcome of the dynamics of criminal groups on their way to claiming territory and dominion over routes for the movement of drugs across the border to the United States: "la plaza." But the specific form of annihilation seen in the two semiotically linked events: first, the victim, decapitated and hung from a bridge, and second, the execution of a journalist, made visible the kinds of violence to which Cavarero refers, with the exposition of the inert victim, like a sort of trophy and threat, at the same time, with implications for both the city itself and the circulation of information in that space.

MEXICAN HORRORISM

I think I'd better not tell you where I was trained because that could be danger-
ous, but what I can tell you is that when we finished the jobs, we almost always
went to los Filtros, out in Camargo, Chihuahua [a natural mineral spring and
popular bathing spot]. (Alex)

Alex, as well as other *sicarios* interviewed for this book, spoke of receiving
training in areas far outside the city, where they learned how to use different calibers of firearms, as well as strategies and tactics to prepare them to
know when to flee, and how to hit their mark with a minimum of mistakes.

Such is the case of Edgar Jiménez Lugo, "El Ponchis," a teenage *sicario*
born in San Diego, California, but raised in Mexico from the age of five,
who became a media celebrity upon his arrest in 2010 (see also Chap. 3).
At age 14, when he was detained, he was an integral member of the
Pacífico Sur cartel. His sister was the romantic partner of his boss, Julio de
Jesús Hernández Radilla, known as El Negro, who was the organization's
chief sicario and the one in charge of disposing of bodies. El Ponchis
learned to torture, mutilate and assassinate his victims through a military
style training regimen in which he was required to march and do field
exercises, and would be beaten and confined if he didn't comply with
orders. These training programs were delivered in rural or remote mountain areas where recruits spent three months learning discipline, weaponry,
and effective forms of torture. This youth spent only three years in prison
because by Mexican law a minor between ages 14 and 16 cannot be
detained longer. After his release in 2013 he was repatriated to the United
States (CBS News 11/27/2013: https://www.cbsnews.com/news/
teen-drug-cartel-hitman-freed-in-mexico-deported-to-the-us/).

In contemporary Mexico, violent scenarios unfurl every day all over the
country, some more terrible than others, but each with its own traits that
taken together sketch out imaginaries of a fractured society. The not so
distant reality that the center of the country lived out on October 2, 1968
with the massacre of student movement protesters, and more recently on
September 26, 2014 in Iguala, Guerrero, in which 43 students of the
Ayotzinapa Rural Teachers' College were disappeared, does not in any
way diminish the lamentable acts that occurred in between, among them
the flaying of Julio César, a student enrolled in the rural Raúl Isidro Burgos
school; the assassination of Juanelo, the son of poet Javier Sicilia; the massacres of Villas de Salvárcar (Ciudad Juárez, Chihuahua), San Fernando

(Tamaulipas), and Tierra Blanca (Guerrero); the 120 plus journalists murdered between 2000 and 2018; and the rising index of impunity—69.21 in 2018, the highest level in the Americas (LeClercq Ortega and Rodríguez-Sánchez Lara 7).

The Villas de Salvárcar massacre of Ciudad Juárez (which we recounted in our Introduction) hit the city particularly hard. This incident, an armed assault on a private party on January 31, 2010, resulted in the death of 15 students who were not the targets of the killers (see Lachica Huerta). Villas de Salvárcar was apparently nothing more than a mistake. A group of teenage students organized a party to celebrate the birthday of one of the members of the Jaguars soccer team of Centro de Bachillerato Tecnológico Industrial y Servicios (commonly known as CBTIS) High School in Ciudad Juárez, which competes in what is known as the AA league. Most of those in attendance were teenage students who attended CBTIS or other local schools. The party was held in a relatively low income neighborhood of which many residents were employed in local maquiladoras. That night several trucks transported a dozen gunmen who, in less than eight minutes, shot mercilessly at the young people who were there celebrating. An investigation concluded that "The Line," an armed wing of the Juárez cartel, confused the AA football league with a rival armed contingency known as Artistas Asesinos, also commonly referred to as AA. For many, this massacre marked a milestone for the city, making clear that the increasingly rampant violence had spread far beyond the domain of rival narcotics syndicates provoking a visit of Mexican president Felipe Calderón to the city.

In the context of Ciudad Juárez, it was a combination of the visibility of the violence (bodies hung from bridges, tossed into public thoroughfares), its horrific nature (signs of torture, chopped off body parts, decapitations), and its spread into venues of everyday life having nothing to do with those in engaged in battle that left the city terrified. It was not only bystanders who were in the wrong place at the time of an assassination, but victims targeted by mistake. If many people had already stopped leaving their houses except for the most essential activities, fears were now heightened and universalized. Following the Salvárcar massacre, Juárez would endure an average of nearly ten homicides per day in 2010, up from a little over four in 2008 and 7.5 in 2009, a record high that stands to this day.

Cavarero analyzes those acts that people might understand as inhuman in themselves, including mutilations, decapitations, and acts of torture, or as inhuman undertakings enacted by irrational beings, where their irrationality is like that normally attributed to animals. Animal acts lack reason, but inhuman acts, she argues, are different, and it is difficult not to attribute them to forces of evil. Executions and acts of torture or mutilation, according to Cavarero, are premeditated tasks that have been thought out and rationalized by humans. Cruelty as an evil act has its objective of causing injury, pain or psychological trauma that may apply only to the victim, but may also inflict suffering far beyond the context of the torture chamber or murder scene. It may not end with death itself, but rather with the exhibition of death, the public display of the inert victim, which may provoke widespread fear and intensify the suffering of loved ones.

The idea of Juárez being the most dangerous city in the world, even more perilous than conflict zones in war torn countries like Afghanistan, Iraq or Syria, was bolstered by the messages communicated in national and international media, which reported assiduously on the sensational display of cadavers, following with reiterations of official discourse on the intensified war against the narcos, but in some cases with journalism serving unequivocally as propaganda for criminal groups that had developed chains of influence in news media organizations. On many occasions delinquent groups would take advantage of news media infrastructure, performing executions during broadcast hours; in that way, with competition for ratings, news programs conceded air time to these acts, for example exhibiting the narcos' messages on canvas tarps, sheets or cardboard posters, and guaranteeing wide dissemination. There were even transmissions that would go live minutes after pubic executions in high impact locations, showing images of their viciousness, such as dismemberments or other mutilations, as exemplified in headlines such as "Mexico Man's Face Skinned and Stitched onto a Soccer Ball in Sinaloa in Threat to Juarez Drug Cartel" (New York Daily News 1/9/2010: https://www.nydailynews.com/news/world/mexico-man-face-skinned-stitched-soccer-ball-sinaloa-threat-juarez-drug-cartel-article-1.181143). In this way, the violence spread from the public places where it occurred to people's living rooms. Each crime scene was conceived as a form of communication between rival groups, but also performed an assertion of power that demanded the submission of the government and the general public. The homicides became a blog to which audiences awaited updates on the relationships of submission and domination, and later annihilation, stories in which evil was an essential plot device. However, these were not stories of good versus evil, but rather inside stories from within the realm of evil itself, of narcos versus narcos, in which the audience waited to find out who would win, to which consortium of evil society would need to submit.

Evil is a condition that, according to Philip Zimbardo "consists in intentionally behaving in ways that harm, abuse, demean, dehumanize, or destroy innocent others – or using one's authority and systemic power to encourage or permit others to do so on your behalf" (5). This definition enters in conflict with the acts of people like Alex, who, as we will see, are convinced that their rivals or opponents deserve to die, and therefore are not innocent, but rather are enemies who have assaulted the interests of their group, which becomes the main justification for their acts.

Zimbardo's book, *The Lucifer Effect*, moves from the banality of evil (Arendt) to the banality of heroism, which implies the capacity "to uphold what is best in human nature," to resist social influences "as the profound assertion of human dignity opposing evil" (xiv). Sicarios would appear to behave in distinct opposition to banal heroism. However, their relationship with evil is also distinct from Zimbardo's emblematic case study, the 1971 Stanford prison experiment, which revealed that anyone can be a promotor of evil, that a person only needs to be exposed to specific circumstances in order to "activate" the sinister side of their nature, which could lead them to kill, whether for survival or not, it is often assumed that sicarios do not develop critical thought about nor recognize errors in their actions. Indeed most sicarios are recruited when young and impressionable, often during their adolescence, as was the case with el Ponchis and with Alex. However, the Lucifer effect, which is situational, and therefore temporary, is insufficient to explain the mindset of Mexico's sicarios, who kill repeatedly and often, should they survive, over long periods of time.

THE POWER OF HORROR

For Arendt, to speak of violence requires speaking of power, as there is no better manifestation of power than that which hurls forth from the barrel of a firearm, whether the shooter is a police officer or a gangster. For Alex, the sensation of firing a gun was, without a doubt, a display of power.

> *I felt it, too: sometimes your fingers just stick on the trigger and you don't let it go, I don't know why. In a blaze of gunfire, you don't feel it happening. You know you have power, you have everything. And if you feel like the big guy, nothing can stop you, and then your finger sticks to the trigger until you've emptied the magazine.* (Alex)

The mindset known as agonistic disposition, that of killing or being killed, intensifies in the moment of the act, that of killing, of perhaps conquering, and of not dying. The flare of the gunshot that ends someone's life is the equivalent of winning, of both taking a life and taking in a salary. It is a challenge posed as a power struggle in which the act of killing is a duty in the form annihilation. Annihilation communicates a message of force and domination of one group over another. It is a strategy that aims for absolute power, which at the level of the assassin may be assimilated not only as a momentary domination of one individual over another, but as a more enduring collective supremacy.

For Michel Foucault, power doesn't necessarily have to do with the exercise of domination, but rather is a dynamic that can be visualized as a web of relations that moves through bodies. The power of paid assassins can be understood literally, when they murder their victims, as the power of domination or annihilation; but Foucault's notion of power reveals the complexity of the sicarios' position beyond the moment of the kill. Within the greater assemblage of their livelihoods, sicarios are far from powerful. That is to say that sicarios play both roles: the dominant, at the instant they carry out their tasks, but also the dominated when they assume their place at the service of an illicit group. Where sicarios end up in this war are as operatives of domination, subjects of economic structures, and of the power exercised by drug trafficking organizations, both in their struggles against rival organizations, and in their endeavors to resist state efforts to control or eliminate them. In this Foucauldian formulation, war crosses boundaries moving into and within the structures of the state, and into and within the groups and individuals that manifest these power relations. Any feelings of power experienced by a sicario as adrenaline at the moment of an execution coexist with sensations sustained by internal hierarchies that may be more persistent, but may also be unstable in a volatile context in which death is an everyday occurrence in the workplace.

Writings about evil often refer back paradigmatically to the crimes of the Holocaust, and more recently to acts of terrorism. Nonetheless, approaches to evil are complicated by the difficulties in defining it, as it is difficult to think about evil without limiting the question to a negative act, such as a crime defined by a criminal code. But questioning beyond the surface, answers begin losing clarity, and often when reason prevails over emotion, evil simply doesn't fit the broader context of the act. Zygmunt Bauman writes: "The question, 'what is evil' is unanswerable because what we tend to call 'evil' is precisely the kind of wrong which we can neither understand nor even clearly articulate, let alone explain its presence to our full satisfaction" (Bauman, *Liquid Fear* 54).

In his *Modernity and Holocaust*, Bauman assumes that the dissonance between the rationality of the actor and the rationality of the action are the causes of historical events like those emerging from Nazism. Whether or not they overlap or coincide, neither rationality depends on the actor; instead, they emanate from the scenario of action, and in equal measure depend on factors beyond the actor's control. In other words, the genocidal events of the Holocaust were orchestrated by the powers of the Nazi state, which is what controlled the situation (i.e., a handful of individuals). In the case of the sicarios, this authority is represented by the cartels, institutions that operate in the margins of the powers of the state. Extrapolating further, the scenario is the prevailing market of moving drugs to the neighboring country; the action is the war over control of routes and markets among the cartels, while the factor outside of their control is the fight that the state wages against them. Bauman draws on the results of Stanley Milgram's notorious 1974 empirical experiment that, designed in the wake of the Eichmann trial, sought to measure the disposition of participants to obey the orders of an authority even when the acts they obediently commit may come into conflict with their personal conscience. Milgram's experiment concludes that cruel acts are not perpetrated by cruel individuals, but rather by ordinary men or women who seek success in life, in the end demonstrating that inhumanity emerges from social relations and how they are rationalized.

THE CASE OF ALEX

I met Alex at the Escuela Mexico, a juvenile detention center in Ciudad Juárez in 2013, just after the three consecutive years that this border city had been designated the most dangerous in the world, with an annual rate of homicides per 100,000 inhabitants ranging from 191 to 229. He was nineteen years old at that time, and would qualify as an adult within Mexican criminal law. But he had been arrested as a juvenile, and because of his age was not sent to prison. He looked like an ordinary teenager; he was pale, short hair, smooth skinned, without signs of a beard. His appearance communicated nothing more than his age: he was a teenager. He was skinny, not at all brawny, of medium height. His facial features were fine, his gaze was attentive. He approached me and told me his name and his aspirations:

I'll get out in two years. I was a good kid. I went off track, but I want to go on studying something in electronics. I want to get out and start a family. I want to see my little sister, and my family. I'm different now. Before I was very impulsive; now I want to get married and have a couple daughters.

Like many young people of his age, who are learning a trade, going to college, starting a family, Alex was planning for his future. It might be said that he had his whole life ahead of him.

But he had already lived a whole range of harrowing experiences, and committed a copious number of atrocious acts that will undoubtedly burden him the rest of his life. He apparently thought a lot about his future, not only with hope, but also with serious trepidation:

I need to be alert because everything in this life has its consequences. I don't know what is going to happen, but I don't believe I'm going to heaven. I've gotten used to the idea that I'm going to get killed. But they haven't messed with my family. I have a repeating dream. In my dream I'm watching myself, and then I feel that my dead body comes rising up toward me.

Alex worked several years in the business and although he always took care that they didn't learn his name and true identity, he is afraid that they'll look for him when he is released. He entered the trade because he was tired of depending on his mother for money. She worked all day in Ciudad Juárez while he went to a school located in El Valle de Juárez, outside the city. One day at a party he met some adults who told him about making some fast money by following orders. At first he was assigned to round up some livestock along the border near the El Porvenir-Fort Hancock crossing, and then near the Caseta-Fabens border bridge. The real objective was to move cocaine across; they would herd the animals a few meters across the border onto the US side at a place where there's no wall or river physically dividing the territories. Before getting caught by the border patrol, the packages would be dropped at specific hiding places, buried or otherwise camouflaged so that they could later be retrieved by people on the other side using GPS technologies. If the kids herding the livestock got caught, they would pretend to have gotten lost and go straight back to the Mexican side. Each package successfully delivered could earn between 10,000 and 30,000 pesos (500 to 1500 dollars).

The range of job types within a cartel is quite broad, and those who do well with simpler tasks can be promoted up the ranks. However, more lucrative positions might also be significantly more risky. If detention by border patrol agents for smuggling might cause some discomfort, promotion to the rank of sicario implies living under constant threat. A small mistake might mean sudden death. But a successful result, which can gain points with the boss, might lead to a bonus (cash, drugs, vacation trips, women) paid out to reward dedication and productivity.

So then in the office we put on some gear; if it was a big job that might hit snags, we'd dress in special outfits, uniforms of federal police or soldiers – we'd have the full getup. Sometimes we'd smoke a joint, although I didn't like to because it would make me sleepy. And others would do a line, but I really didn't like that either. I preferred to be totally alert, and being drugged is not the same, as I see it. Once we'd seen the route, we'd plan our return. We'd almost always go in two or three pickups – in our cell there'd be five or six of us in different pickups: one was almost always designated to do the job, and the others would watch the perimeter and the weaker flanks, be ready with the frequencies and times. We were really well organized, and always did a good job – that's how the boss liked it (Alex).

MURDER IN MEXICO

Although Mexico has had a violent history, and some, such as Elena Azaola, consider violent conflict to be part of the nation's cultural baggage, a deep seated legacy, cartel violence is quite different from the violence of, say, the Mexican war of independence or its revolution, events that evoke national pride. Nonetheless, the nation's long history of violence can be thought in some ways as having led up to today's carnage. For Azaola there are three basic forms of violence in Mexico. First there are deeply ingrained cultural patterns of violence, that date back centuries and have no direct links to criminal groups, but whose logics might justify otherwise unacceptable behaviors, and in that way contribute to increased levels of violence in recent decades. The second category has to do with weakened and broken institutions charged with security, law enforcement and criminal justice—which have led to breakdowns in the administration of justice, and translated to elevated levels of impunity, an absence of rule of law. The third involves the quality of social and economic policies, which exacerbate gaps in inequality and vulnerability. In consequence: "Today we must deal with spiraling violence that is difficult to contain and whose repercussions we'll be enduring for many years to come" (Azaola 29).

For Rossana Reguillo, today's scenes of bloodshed and cruelty present a grammar of violence "that draws attention to an ontological relation between violent – universal – death and a dismembered and shattered – particular – body" (*Culturas juveniles* 34). From this perspective, she questions the new standards in exercising violence, where power, whether of criminal syndicates or the state itself, needs to be violently inscribed onto bodies. Capitalism promotes what she calls an "accelerated disconnect," in which scenarios and symbols of order dissipate ("Legitimidad(es) divergentes").

Alex's story lays out the ways in which young Mexican men, both teenagers and young adults, might be drawn into what seems like a naturalized landscape of violence.

> *Young people grow up fast, and they are disastrous, especially in Juárez. The country is all fucked up. Kids get into drug trafficking because they get harassed into it, because their families don't have any money, out of revenge, or because they love to fight.* (Alex)

For Alex, entry into the sicario trade was not comfortable. He recalls his early days, and one scene in particular in which the victim had been smoking when he was killed:

> *I think the first two or three were different. If you drank water, it tasted different – who knows why this job is strange. The cigarette, because it's strange, I was looking at the bloody cigarette, and I felt strange, as if little by little I was smoking his blood.* (Alex)

Only when he spoke about smoking his victim's bloodied cigarette did he pause, without expressing more details, implying that this moment was a turning point in his life as a sicario. Indeed, before long, Alex adapted to a new lifestyle that offered him a number of advantages:

> *It starts to feel normal. If they tell you you're going out for this job, no worries, you just grab them by the hair, fast, and with those knives they use for cutting limes you quickly slit their throat. I cut about five throats with that knife; it was the one that the guys fought over: "Where's the knife, where is it?" they'd say. And I liked it, too. It depends on how you do it. Sometimes they stare at you telling you not to do it. But it's better to have them kneeling down so they can't see you, and gagged because if they don't have something in their mouth, they scream a lot, and then if you're high on something, it'll give you a bad trip.*

An Ethics of Cruelty

Viciousness refers to deliberately cruel behavior, sometimes borne in anger. Cruelty implies inflicting unnecessary pain or suffering on others in order to provoke an emotional response of pleasure; the American Psychiatric Association catalogues cruelty as a psychological disorder. The actions of sicarios in the years under scrutiny here in Ciudad Juárez might begin with torture and mutilation, continue with murder, and then culminate in the exhibition of the remains in a public venue. These acts seem to be profoundly evil, vicious, and cruel, yet they appear not to perturb their perpetrators as they blithely reference them, citing gratuitous justifications.

In the case of Alex, his descriptions of the viciousness of many of his crimes help to understand how he could normalize not only the idea of being an assassin, but that of being a good or bad one. With calm and stoicism Alex indicated that before long he started to enjoy his job as a sicario; he came to like killing and to get pleasure from doing it. He felt he had developed a style in carrying out his executions.

> When you're letting loose a barrage of bullets, you don't feel it – you know you've got the power, you've got it all. You feel like a big shot, like nothing can stop you. And then you keep your finger on the trigger until you've spent all the bullets – it's just a few seconds. Later on you develop your own way of executing, and mine was breaking them in two, lengthwise, from top to bottom, I'd shoot them up and down, from top to bottom, dividing them into two. (Alex)

The *sicario* interviewed by Charles Bowden for an article first published in *Harper's* in 2009 differentiates between two classes of assassins working in Mexican criminal drug enterprises: "He [...] resents people who like to kill. They are not professional. Real sicarios kill for money. But there are people who kill for fun" (184). Bowdin's sicario is adamant about the difference: "People will say, 'I haven't killed anyone for a week'. So they'll go out and kill someone. This kind of person does not belong in your unit, you kill them. The people you really want are [...] trained killers" (184). Perhaps this professional element—"It's a kind of work, you follow orders" (Bowden 178)—produces a distance between the person, a professional, a laborer, and the evil act.

The notion of evil is one that comes up again and again in chatting with Alex and the other interviewees. They understand evil, they have an idea of evil as a concept, but they don't fully grasp that they might be considered inherently evil for what they do. Killing in self-defense is legally distinct from a case of reckless manslaughter, which in turn differs from a premeditated homicide. For many sicarios, these are not relevant categories; instead, it just comes down to killing or being killed. Much social science literature, indeed much social infrastructure from systems of criminal justice to religious apparatuses of penance, assumes cruelty as a characteristic in acts committed by evildoers, accountable agents of evil who deserve a punishment (Ovejero), a logic that is not always evident in testimonial narratives of sicarios.

Hermann Herlinghaus's study of narcoculture seeks to address the tension between the social conditions that seem to generate "dramatic forms of labor" (12) such as that carried out by paid assassins, and the social systems that hold fast to infrastructures designed to punish evildoers. The laborers in drug trafficking organizations, often casually referred to as "narcos," are generally thought to be both inherently evil people (when viewed from the perspectives of the damage they wreak), and unfortunate individuals simply struggling to provide for their families (when contemplated from their personal backgrounds). However, what is perhaps most difficult to accept from the latter perspective is that narcos seem often to accept the realm of drug trafficking, and the extraordinarily cruel violence that it implies, as a viable option – without moral qualms (118–20). This context in which the sicarios themselves as well as those around them (their families or friends who benefit from their work) might become conditioned to accept or even embrace "violence without guilt" (130) presents a major ethical dilemma for our times.

However, the question of guilt, linked forcefully to notions of evil and evildoing, comes up frequently in testimonial narratives of paid assassins of Mexican drug trafficking organizations. In celebrated journalist Javier Valdez Cárdenas's interviews with sicarios, it is a prominent theme. One sicario insists, "we are not evil people, we only administer justice on those who deserve it" (22). However, another of Valdez Cárdenas's interviewees, despite repeating over and over "I'm not evil" (181), declares that he takes responsibility for his actions: "I'm to blame for everything" (189). The journalist describes a scene of this sicario, referred to as El Rey, looking into a mirror and stating "It's me, it was me" and then "asking God for forgiveness" (189). The sicario interviewed by Charles Bowden and whose story is told in Bowden's *Murder City* also insists, "We are not monsters [...] We have education, we have feelings" (178). However, the fact that he refuses to see himself as evil does not mean that he does not experience feelings of guilt for his actions. After leaving the cartel, he reevaluates his life and changes direction. As he puts it, "God saved me. I repented" (222). Ultimately he admits, "I remain a terrible person, but now I have God on my side" (223).

The interventions of God into the stories of the latter two assassins entail something of a battle of good and evil within their own psyches, implying that they are not inherently evil individuals, but that, perhaps following Christian doctrine, evil entered their lives, tempting them to transgress, and defined their acts, but not their souls. This same Christian doctrine offers a path for redemption that might not be so easily obtained under legal codes—or public opinion. One of the assassins quoted in the Valdez Cárdenas collection of stories from the world of Mexican drug violence, referred to as Mario, recounts that his "jefe" frequently quoted the Bible. After a particularly bloody assassination, *el jefe* commented that "'everything was fucked up' because people had stopped reading the Bible and believing in God"; he articulated his personal goals in conquering territories of rival groups in this way: "they'll all go to fuck and they'll all learn the Bible" (21).

A WAY OF LIFE

Alex relates his experiences casually, as others his age might talk about sporting events or weekend excursions: with some emotion, but with a nonchalance that reflects normality. Unlike some other sicarios, who might never cease to struggle to stomach the violence that came to characterize their everyday lives, he took it all in, assimilated it and learned to align it with his emotional life:

Sometimes, I tell you, if you have to get high on something, you've missed out. Because it destresses you a whole lot. A lot of times if you're angry or are dealing with a problem from home, you can get over it by killing someone, killing your troubles right along with your target. I think that at one point I became addicted to killing because instead of them calling me for a job, I would call them and tell them, I'd ask for work. And they'd say "uh, there's nobody to knock off." Because I'd wake up, I'd act weird, all because I wanted to kill someone. It became a vice for me – how can I say it, you get addicted.

Alex's taste for blood grew, and in less than a year he was able to amass dozens of victims. Although he had no interest in keeping a log, his worst acts gave him some satisfaction, along with his weekly salary that he shared with him mother who told him she preferred not to ask where it was coming from.

However, he also admits that his highly volatile work life did not lend itself to a psychological equilibrium, as anything could happen at any time. He became noticeably upset, biting his lip, when he confessed the following:

> *Once I was involved in an operation: there were two cells and a shootout, a big deal. There I killed my grandfather, my stepfather's dad. It was a stray bullet. I didn't know he was nearby, but that afternoon I found out he'd died. He had nothing to do with the gunfire. That night I was eating some pozole and it made me nauseous because I was imagining the blood, and I wanted to vomit.*

A Bad End

Alex lived a few incredibly intense years. He claims to have killed some 50 people before his arrest at age sixteen. He explains further:

> *There were a lot of people because some were group operatives, but I did knock off more than fifty myself. The truth is that I don't keep count; there's no point – there are a lot of them. Sometimes I did it in a barrage of gunfire, in a big bunch, and I don't count those. If I did, there would be more.*

All this occurred between ages 14 and 16, when he was arrested, tried, and sentenced. He was convicted for a double homicide in which he says he was careless. His sentence was 11 years, but since he was tried as a minor, he'll be released after serving five years, in accordance with Mexican juvenile justice law. He assesses things in this way: "I wouldn't change anything in my life. There's a reason why I have this destiny. But when I get out I'll try harder."

Conclusion

When asked whether he saw himself as "good, bad or regular," Alex responded, unequivocally: "Good." He recognizes that he has not always acted as he should: "I was reckless for a while," and fears consequences deep into his future: "I don't believe I'm going to go to heaven." He sees himself as a good person who has done bad things.

Indeed, none of the individuals interviewed see themselves as inherently evil. Several describe some sicarios as basically "good people" (Rosina) or even "very good people" (Tony), emphasizing positive characteristics such as respectfulness, loyalty and generosity. Others separate their core identities from their jobs: they did what they needed to do to get ahead (Alberto), or that their job implied good and bad things, like any other job (Raúl). And several insist that no one should have the right to make these kinds of absolute judgements, insisting that "only the one up there can judge me; he decides the gravity" of my acts (Tony). One even asserts, "my God has already forgiven me, yes, he's forgiven me for everything" (Salmo).

At the same time, it was not necessarily difficult for these same sicarios to see other narcos as evil: "It is bad if you have the evil intention to indoctrinate more people [...] Selling drugs, well you know you're harming a lot more innocent people, including children" (Tony). As mentioned in the previous chapter, some, like Anastasio, even justify their own brutality in the evil of their rivals, who "were nearly always [...] kidnappers, extortionists, rapists [...], people who killed children, women." Anastasio's boss instilled in his group of sicarios the belief that they were performing a kind of social cleansing, knocking off the evildoers of the rival cartel, while at the same time themselves carrying out their violent acts under a moral code: "we didn't kill innocent women and children."

Tony's rationalization: "if it's to help people who need it, even if you do it, you're doing a good deed" contrasts significantly with Alex's articulation, cited above, of his addiction to killing. Alex, who does not make any claims to doing good deeds, further explains the kind of work that gave him the most pleasure:

> *If I killed them just like that, I wasn't satisfied – unless there was a chase. And if we had to just kill them at once, and had to shrug it off, I couldn't just do it [...] I just didn't feel good and would get really bummed out* (Alex).

It's hard to discern where the line between good and evil lies in cases like that of Alex, a teenager who confesses to becoming addicted to killing and especially enjoys unhurried, methodical forms of killing, while seeing himself as an inherently good person, in whose life experience of poverty many might find justifications for his moral derailment.

If Baudrillard's proposal that the only way to distinguish convincingly between good and evil is through superstition, like much postmodernist thinking, seems inadequate when aligned with lived reality, after listening to the stories and assessments of sicarios, we believe that any casual assignation of evil or wickedness, even to a context abhorrent as that of the extreme violence experienced in Ciudad Juárez around the year 2010, also falls flat, the apparent product of emotional reaction or lazy reasoning. Labeling a person as evil harks back to nineteenth century positivist criminology, and lends itself to dangerous racializations and expressions of xenophobic animosity. The first step in solving the problem of contemporary narcoviolence is understanding the motivations of the protagonists and perpetuators of this violence.

Colombian Alonso Salazar published his seminal book *No nacimos pa'semilla*, in 1991, recording a series of testimonial narratives of young sicarios from Medellín. More than 20 years later, the general rubric of the personal stories narrated by Mexican sicarios, while always introducing new perspectives and varying degrees of atrocity, is not much different, and yet the stories continue to be shocking.

Bauman's metaphor of liquidity, as laid out in the work of his later years, suggests that forms of life that were once solid have assumed a new state, meaning that the symbols and values that preconceive their existence have also changed. Late capitalism has diluted what was once solid: institutions that seemed immovable, built on deep and solid foundations, have evolved in a context of unbridled consumption. In this way postmodernity operates based on desires that must be fulfilled, turned into an asset, sometimes in scenarios of life or death stakes. Humanity has been banalized—not only deconstructed but commodified to the point of being considered disposable, like any other product. The horrific acts of sicarios seem, like the realm of what has been called necropolitics, to exemplify this contemporary condition, but it remains to come up with a definition of evil that unambiguously accounts for their individual psychological trajectories.

WORKS CITED

Alvarado Vázquez, Ramón Ismael. "El buchón: ¿una imagen juvenil o una expresión cultural urbana de Sinaloa?" *Tla-Melaua: Revista de Ciencias Sociales* 11.42, 2017: 136–57.

Andreas, Peter. *Smuggler Nation: How Illicit Trade Made America*. New York: Oxford University Press, 2013.

Anzaldúa, Gloria. *Borderlands/La Frontera: The New Mestiza*. San Francisco: Aunt Lute Books, 1987.

Appel, Marco. "Ante el Estado fallido, narcoestado sustituto." *Proceso* 1853, 2012: 36–38.

Arendt, Hannah. *Eichmann in Jerusalem: A Report on the Banality of Evil* [1963]. New York: Penguin, 2006.

———. *On Violence*. New York: Harcourt Brace Javanovich, 1970.

Astorga Almanza, Luis Alejandro. *Mitología del "narcotraficante" en México*. Mexico City: Universidad Nacional Autónoma de México/Plaza y Valdés, 1995.

Azaola, Elena. "La violencia de hoy, la violencia de siempre." *Desacatos* 40, 2012: 13–32.

Bataillon, Gilles, "Narcotráfico y corrupción: las formas de la violencia en México en el siglo XXI." *Nueva Sociedad* 255, 2015: 54–68.

Baudrillard, Jean. *The Intelligence of Evil or the Lucidity Pact* [2004], Chris Turner, Trans. Oxford: Berg, 2005.

Bauman, Zygmunt. *Does Ethics Have a Chance in a World of Consumers?* Cambridge: Harvard University Press, 2008.

———. *Liquid Fear*. Malden, MA: Polity Press, 2006.

———. *Liquid Modernity*. Cambridge: Polity Press, 2000a.

© The Author(s), under exclusive license to Springer Nature Switzerland AG 2022
A. Chacón Castañón, R. M. Irwin, *Listening to Sicarios*, New Directions in Latino American Cultures,
https://doi.org/10.1007/978-3-030-94118-5

————. *Modernity and the Holocaust* [1989]. Ithaca, NY: Cornell University Press, 2000b.

Becerra Romero, América Tonantzin and Diego Armando Hernández Cruz. "Fascinación por el poder: consumo y apropiación de la narcocultura por jóvenes en contextos de narcotráfico." *Intersticios Sociales* 17, 2019: 259–85.

Beck, Ulrich. *Risk Society: Toward a New Modernity.* London: Sage, 1992.

Benítez Manaut, Raúl. "La crisis de seguridad en México." *Nueva Sociedad* 220, 2009: 173–89.

Benjamin, Walter. "Critique of Violence" [1921]. *Selected Writings,* Vol. I. Cambridge, MA: Belknap Press, 1996: 236–52.

Berman, Marshall. *All That Is Solid Melts Into Air: The Experience of Modernity* [1982]. New York: Penguin, 1988.

Blog del Narco, *Dying for the Truth: Undercover Inside the Mexican Drug War.* Port Townsend, Washington: Feral House, 2013.

Bourdieu, Pierre. *Masculine Domination* [1998]. Trans. Richard Nice. Stanford: Stanford University Press, 2001.

————. *Sociología y Cultura.* México, D.F. : Grijalbo, 1990.

Bowden, Charles. *Murder City: Ciudad Juárez and the Global Economy's New Killing Fields.* New York: Nation Books, 2010.

Boyce, Geoffrey, Jeffrey Banister and Jeremy Slack. "You and What Army? Violence, The State, and Mexico's War on Drugs." *Territory, Politics and Governance* 3.4, 2015: 446–68.

Campbell, Howard and Tobin Hansen. "Is Narco-Violence in Mexico Terrorism?" *Bulletin of Latin American Research* 33.2, 2014: 158–73.

Carrión, Fernando. "El sicariato: ¿un homicidio calificado?" *Urvio: Revista Latinoamericana de Seguridad Ciudadana* 8, 2009: 7–9.

Castel, Robert. *El ascenso de las incertidumbres. Trabajo, protecciones, estatuto del individuo.* Buenos Aires: Fondo de Cultura Económica, 2009.

Cavarero, Adriana. *Horrorismo: nombrando la violencia contemporánea* [2007]. Saleta de Salvador Agra, Trans. Barcelona/Mexico City: Anthropos Editorial/ Universidad Autónoma Metropolitana, Iztapalapa, 2009.

Cisneros, José Luis and Mitzi Elizabeth Robles Rodríguez. "Violencia y muerte: entre la narrativa de la crueldad y el horror: las iconografías de la criminalidad juvenil." *Revista Internacional de Ciencias del Estado y de Gobierno* 1.3, 2018: 451–69.

Córdova Plaza, Rosío and Ernesto Hernández Sánchez. "En la línea de fuego: construcción de masculinidades en jóvenes tamaulipecos ligados al narco." *Revista de Dialectología y Tradiciones Populares* 71.2, 2016: 559–77.

Coronil, Fernando. "Listening to the Subaltern: The Poetics of Neocolonial States." *Poetics Today* 15.4, 1994: 643–58.

Corvera Quevedo, Luis Javier and José de Jesús Lara Ruiz. *Narcotráfico e identidad juvenil.* Culiacán: Universidad Autónoma de Sinaloa, 2012.

Cruz Sierra, Salvador. "Violencia social y homicidio doloso en Ciudad Juárez: poder, crueldad y goce de una masculinidad temeraria." Miguel Olmos Aguilera, Comp. *Fronteras culturales, alteridad y violencia*. Tijuana: El Colegio de la Frontera Norte, 2013: 293–316.

———. "Violencia y jóvenes: pandilla e identidad masculina en Ciudad Juárez." *Revista Mexicana de Sociología* 76.4, 2014: 613–37.

——— and Luis Ernesto Cervera Gómez. "El homicidio masculino y su georreferenciación." Luis Ernesto Cervera Gómez and Julia Monárrez Fragosa, Coords. *Geografía de la violencia en Ciudad Juárez, Chihuahua*. Tijuana: El Colegio de la Frontera Norte, 2013: 115–144.

D'Ávila, Patricia. "La guerra perdida." *El Cotidiano* 164: 2010, 41–46.

Dávila León, Óscar. "Adolescencia y juventud: de las nociones a los abordajes." *Última Década* 21, 2004: 83–104.

Dear, Michael. *Why Walls Won't Work: Repairing the US-Mexico Divide*. New York: Oxford University Press, 2013.

Echarri Cánovas, Carlos Javier and Julieta Pérez Amador. "El tránsito hacia la adultez: eventos en el curso de vida de los jóvenes en México." *Estudios Demográficos y Urbanos* 22.1, 2006: 43–77.

Eiss, Paul. "Front Lines and Back Channels: The Fractal Publics of *El Blog del Narco*". Paul Gillingham, Michael Lettierri and Benjamin Smith, eds. *Journalism, Satire, and Censorship in Mexico*. Albuquerque: University of New Mexico Press, 2018: 333–52.

Encinas Garza, José Luis. "Jóvenes sicarios: la generación desechable: vivir rápido y morir joven." *Ciencia Universidad Autónoma de Nuevo León* 19.80, 2016: 59–65.

Fazio, Carlos. *Estado de emergencia: de la guerra de Calderón a la guerra de Peña Nieto*. Mexico City: Grijalbo, 2016.

Foucault, Michel. *The History of Sexuality*, Vol. I [1976]. Robert Hurley, Trans. New York: Pantheon Books, 1978.

Fox, James Alan and Jack Levin. *Overkill: Mass Murder and Serial Killing Exposed*. New York: Plenum Press, 1994.

Galtung, Johan. *Tras la violencia, 3R: reconstrucción, reconciliación, resolución. Afrontando los efectos visibles e invisibles de la guerra y la violencia*. Bilbao: Gernika Gogoratuz, 1998.

Garzón, Juan Carlos. *Mafia & Co.: The Criminal Networks in Mexico, Brazil, and Colombia*. Washington, DC: Woodrow Wilson International Center for Scholars, Latin American Program, 2008.

Gaspar de Alba, Alicia and Georgina Guzmán, eds. *Making a Killing: Femicide, Free Trade, and La Frontera*. Austin: University of Texas Press, 2010.

Giddens, Anthony. *Consecuencias de la modernidad*. Madrid: Alianza, 1997.

———. *La constitución de la sociedad*. Buenos Aires: Amorrortu, 1995.

González Rodríguez, Sergio. *Campo de Guerra*. Barcelona: Anagrama, 2014.

Grayson, George and Samuel Logan. *The Executioner's Men: Los Zetas, Criminal Entrepreneurs and the Shadow State They Created.* New Brunswick: Transaction Publishers, 2012.

Griffin, Roger. *Terrorist's Creed: Fanatical Violence and the Human Need for Meaning.* New York: Palgrave Macmillan, 2012.

Herlinghaus, Hermann. *Violence Without Guilt: Ethical Narratives from the Global South.* New York: Palgrave Macmillan, 2009.

Hine, Christine. *Etnografía virtual.* Barcelona: Editorial UOC, 2004.

Hurtado, Omar and Rosa María García Paz. "El narcotráfico en México como problema transnacional." *Revista Mexicana de Política Exterior* 97, 2013: 35–64.

Irwin, Robert McKee and Guillermo Alonso Meneses, eds. *Humanizando la deportación: informes desde las calles de Tijuana.* Tijuana: El Colegio de la Frontera Norte, forthcoming 2021.

Lachica Huerta, Fabiola. *Shattering the Everyday, Rearranging the Ordinary: The Categories, Temporalities, and Spatial Dimensions of an Acute Event: The Case of the Villas de Salvárcar Massacre.* Doctoral Dissertation. New York: The New School University, 2020.

Langton, Jerry. *Gangland: The Rise of the Mexican Drug Cartels from El Paso to Vancouver.* Missisauga, Ontario: John Wiley & Sons Canada, 2012.

Le Clercq Ortega, Juan Antonio and Gerardo Rodríguez Sánchez Lara. *La impunidad subnacional en México y sus dimensiones.* Puebla: Universidad de las Américas, 2018.

Linares, Adriana. "La leyenda negra." Ciudad Juárez, 2005: http://www.drogas-mexico.org/index.php?nota=244&tipo=6&id_ext=3.

Maffesoli, Michel. *Elogio de la razón sensible: una visión intuitiva del mundo contemporáneo.* Barcelona: Paidós Ibérica, 1998.

Manjón-Cabeza, Araceli. *La solución: La legalización de las drogas.* México: Debate, 2012.

Martín Barbero, Jesús. *Entre saberes desechables y saberes indispensables.* Bogotá: Centro de Competencia en Comunicación para América Latina, 2009.

Martínez, Óscar and Juan José Martínez. *The Hollywood Kid: The Violent Life and Death of an MS-13 Hitman.* John B. Washington and Daniela María Ugaz, trans. London: Verso, 2019.

Méndez, Luis Humberto. *Territorio maquilador y violencia. El caso de Ciudad Juárez.* El Cotidiano, 27–40. 2010.

Mezzadra, Sandro and Brett Neilson. *Border As Method, Or the Multiplication of Labor.* Durham: Duke University Press, 2013.

Milgram, Stanley. "Behavioral Study of Obedience." *Journal of Abnormal and Social Psychology* 67.4, 1963: 371–78.

Mignolo, Walter. *Local Histories/Global Designs: Coloniality, Subaltern Knowledges, and Border Thinking.* Princeton: Princeton University Press, 2000.

————. "'Un paradigma otro': colonialidad global, pensamiento fronterizo y cosmopolitanismo crítico." *Dispositio* 25.52, 2005: 127–46.

Miller, Todd. *Border Patrol Nation: Dispatches from the Front Lines of Homeland Security*. San Francisco: City Lights, 2014.

Molloy, Molly and Charles Bowden, eds. *El Sicario: The Autobiography of a Mexican Assassin*. New York: Nation Books, 2011.

Monárrez Fragoso, Julia. "Ciudad Juárez, tiradero nacional de muertos: entre discurso del guerrero y el caballero." *Debate Feminista* 47, 2013a: 205–34.

————. "Serial Sexual Femicide in Ciudad Juárez, 1993–2001." *Aztlán* 28.4, 2003: 153–78.

————. *Trama de una injusticia: feminicidio sistemático en Ciudad Juárez*. Tijuana: El Colegio de la Frontera Norte, 2013b.

Montoya Arias, Luis Ómar and Juan Antonio Fernández Velásquez. "El narcocorrido en México." *Cultura y Droga* 14.16, 2009: 207–32.

Muehlman, Shaylih. *When I Wear My Alligator Boots: Narco-Culture in the US Mexico Borderlands*. Berkeley: University of California Press, 2014.

Núñez Noriega, Guillermo and Claudia Esthela Espinoza Cid. "El narcotráfico como dispositivo de poder sexo-genérico: crimen organizado, masculinidad y teoría *queer*." *Estudios de Género de El Colegio de México* 3.5, 2017: 90–128

Otamendi, María Alejandra. "Juvenicidio armado: homicidios de jóvenes y armas de fuego en América Latina". *Salud Colectiva* 15, 2019: 1–16.

Ovejero, José. *La ética de la crueldad*. Barcelona: Anagrama, 2012

Padgett, Humberto. *Tamaulipas: la casta de los narcogobernadores: un eastern mexicano*. Mexico City: Ediciones Urano, 2016.

Paz, Octavio. *The Labyrinth of Solitude* [1950]. Lysander Kemp, Trans. New York: Grove Press, 1985.

Pérez Aguirre, Manuel. "La masacre de 72 migrantes en San Fernando, Tamaulipas." Sergio Aguayo Quezada, Coord. *En el desamparo: los Zetas, el Estado, la sociedad y las víctimas de San Fernando, Tamaulipas (2010) y Allende, Coahuila (2011)*. Mexico City: El Colegio de México, 2016: https://eneldesamparo.colmex.mx/images/documentos/anexo-2.pdf.

Pérez Mendoza, Araceli. "Violencia estructural de estado y adolescentes en México." *Rayuela: Revista Iberoamericana sobre Niñez y Juventud en Lucha por sus Derechos*, 9, 2013: http://revistarayuela.ednica.org.mx/article/violencia-estructural-de-estado-y-adolescentes-en-m%C3%A9xico.

Ramírez Pimienta, Juan Carlos. *Cantar a los narcos: voces y versos del narcocorrido*. Mexico City: Planeta, 2011.

————. "El Pablote: una nueva mirada al primer corrido dedicado a un traficante de drogas." *Mitologías Hoy* 14, 2016: 41–56.

————. "Sicarias, buchonas y jefas: perfiles de la mujer en el narcocorrido." *Colorado Review of Hispanic Studies* 8–9, 2010-11: 327–52.

Red por los Derechos de la Infancia en México (REDIM). "Balance anual: infancia y adolescencia en México." Mexico City: REDIM, 2019.

Reguillo, Rossana. *Culturas juveniles: formas políticas del desencanto*. Buenos Aires: Siglo XXI, 2012a.

———. "De las violencias: caligrafía y gramática del horror". *Desacatos* 40, 2012b: 33–46.

———. *Emergencia de Culturas Juveniles. Estrategias del desencanto*. Buenos Aires: Editorial Norma, 2000.

———. "Legitimidad(es) divergentes", en José Antonio Pérez Islas, Coord. *Jóvenes mexicanos. Encuesta Nacional de Juventud 2005*, Mexico City: Instituto Mexicano de la Juventud/Secretaría de Educación Pública, 2007: 75–133.

———. "Las múltiples fronteras de la violencia: jóvenes latinoamericanos entre la precarización y el desencanto." *Pensamiento Iberoamericano* 3, 2008: 205–25.

Reyna, Juan Carlos. *Confesión de un sicario: el testimonio de Drago, lugarteniente de un cártel mexicano*. Mexico City: Grijalbo, 2011.

Ríos, Viridiana. "¿Quién se vuelve narco y por qué? El perfil del narcotraficante mexicano." *Este País*, 2009.

Rivera González, José Guadalupe. "El deterioro del capital social como promotor de la violencia y la delincuencia entre la población del municipio de Rioverde, San Luis Potosí." *Papeles de Población* 22.87, 2016: 103–32.

Salazar, Alonso. *No nacimos pa'semilla: la cultura de las bandas juveniles en Medellín*. Bogotá: Centro de Investigación y Educación Popular, 1990.

Salazar Gutiérrez, Salvador. "Vida y castigo: jóvenes en prisión sentenciados por homicidio en Ciudad Juárez." *Estudios Fronterizos* 17.33, 2016: 11–34.

Scherer García, Julio. *Historias de muerte y corrupción*. Mexico City: Grijalbo, 2011.

Urteaga Castro Pozo, Maritza. "De jóvenes contemporáneos: trendys, emprendedores y empresarios culturales". In Maritza Urteaga Castro Pozo, Francisco Cruces, and Néstor García Canclini, eds. *Jóvenes, culturas urbanas y redes digitales*. Barcelona: Editorial Ariel, Fundación Telefónica, 2012: 24–44.

Valdez Cárdenas, Javier. *Los morros del narco: historias reales de niños y jóvenes en el narcotráfico mexicano*. Mexico City: Aguilar, 2011.

Valdez Castellanos, Guillermo. *Historia del narcotráfico en México: apuntes para entender el crimen organizado*. Mexico City: Proceso, 2013.

Valencia, Sayak. *Capitalismo gore*. Santa Cruz de Tenerife: Melusina, 2010.

Valenzuela Arce, José Manuel. *El futuro ya fue: socioantropología de l@s jóvenes en la modernidad*. Tijuana: El Colegio de la Frontera Norte, 2012a.

———. "Identidades y agrupamientos juveniles". In Ángela Garcés Montoya and Luis. Beltrán Pérez Rojas eds. *Juventud, identidad y comunicación: erpistemología de la comunicación*. Medellín: Universidad de Medellín. 2008: 21–52.

———. *Jefe de jefes: corridos y narcocultura en México*. Tijuana: El Colegio de la Frontera Norte, 2014.

———, coord. *Juvenicidio: Ayotzinapa y las vidas precarias en América Latina y España*. Barcelona/Guadalajara/Tijuana: Ned Ediciones/Instituto Tecnológico de Estudios Superiores de Oriente/El Colegio de la Frontera Norte, 2015a.

————. *Sed de mal: feminicidio, jóvenes y exclusión social.* Tijuana/Monterrey: El Colegio de la Frontera Norte/Universidad Autónoma de Nuevo León, 2012b.

————. "Las voces de la calle... y de las redes sociales, los movimientos juveniles y el proyecto neoliberal". En José Manuel Valenzuela Arce, ed. *El sistema es anti-nosotros: culturas, movimientos y resistencias juveniles.* Ciudad de México: Gedisa. 2015b: 29–69.

Voeten, Teun. *The Mexican Drug Violence Hybrid Warfare, Predatory Capitalism and the Logic of Cruelty.* Bloomington, Indiana: Xlibris, 2020.

Weber, Max. "Politics as a Vocation" [1919]. *The Vocation Lectures.* Indianapolis: Hackett Publishing, 2004: 32–94.

Weissman, Deborah. "The Political Economy of Violence: Toward an Understanding of the Gender-Based Murders of Ciudad Juárez." *North Carolina Journal of International Law and Commerce* 30.4, 2005: 795–867.

Winocur, Rosalía. "Internet en la vida cotidiana de los jóvenes". *Revista Mexicana de Sociología,* 68.3, 2006: 551–580.

Wolfgang, Marvin, and Franco Ferracutti. *La subcultura de la violencia: hacia una teoría criminológica.* México D.F.: Fondo de Cultura Económica, 1982.

Zavala, Oswaldo. *Los cárteles no existen: narcotráfico y cultura en México.* Barcelona: Malpaso, 2018.

Zimbardo, Philip. *The Lucifer Effect: Understanding How Good People Turn Evil.* New York: Random House, 2008.

Index

A
Agency, 98
Army, 91

B
Banality, 103
Belonging, 56–58
Border gnosis, *see* Border thinking
Border industrial complex, 17,
    21–42, 54
Borderscapes, 22–24
Border thinking, 14–15, 37
Buchón, 58, 67

C
Cartels
    Beltrán Leyva cartel, 37
    career paths within, 29–42, 51
    Colombian, 25
    as discursive construct, 25–28
    Gulf cartel, 91
    Juárez cartel, 101
    links to border security
        apparatuses, 26–27
    links to private sector, 26
    nuanced view, 41
    Pacífico Sur cartel, 37, 100
    recruiting, 32–33, 43, 47–49, 51
    role in Border Industrial
        Complex, 22
    Sinaloa cartel, 28, 30, 33–34, 39
    Zetas, 91
Collaborative analysis, 13–14
Criminal syndicates, *see* Cartels
Cruelty, 109–111

D
Drug trafficking
    history of, 28–30
    See also Cartels; Sicarios

E
Emotions, *see* Sentiment
Endriago, 15, 17, 81–82

Evil, 18, 89–114
  and banality, 98–99, 103

F
Fear, 11, 18, 40, 66, 69, 70, 79,
  82–87, 97, 101–102
Feelings, *see* Sentiment
Feminized, 18
Fieldwork protocols, 9
Futurity, 50, 52–53

G
Globalization, 95

H
Horrorism, 99–103

I
Impunity, 26, 101
Internet, 55

J
Juvenicide, 49

K
Kidnapping, 56

L
Liquidity, 44, 55, 57, 105, 114
Listening
  as research method, 12–16

M
Masculinity, 16, 65–87
Mérida Initiative, 24
Modernity, 51

N
Narcocorridos, 31, 59, 68, 78, 90,
  95
Narcoculture, 58, 59, 65–68, 78
Narcostate, 94
Ninis, 56

O
Overkill, 83

P
Postmodernity, 53–54
Power, feelings of, 21, 34, 51, 56–57,
  66–73, 97, 103–104
Precarization, 66
Prison, 34, 39, 79, 83, 100

R
Recklessness, 83–85

S
San Fernando massacre, 75, 91, 100
Securitization, 23
Sentiment, 18, 65–87
Sicarios
  ethnographic interviews with, 9–12
  as labor, 18, 31–41, 52, 96
  leaving the trade, 35–36, 39–40

opportunities in Ciudad Juárez,
30–33, 36, 48–49, 64
recruitment by coerción, 32, 59
redemption of, 35, 53, 111
studies on, 2–4
testimonial narratives, 4–6,
14–16, 45, 114
Smuggling, 22–27, 29, 33, 36, 38

T
Terrorism, 91–92

V
Villas de Salvárcar massacre, 1–2, 75,
100, 101
Violence
in Ciudad Juárez, 6–9, 19, 28–40,
47–49, 54, 74, 89, 101
history in Mexico, 107–108
male on male, 73, 74

masculinity and, 13–14
in narcocorridos, 31
politics of, 26
spectacularized, 89, 102–103
state violence, 92–94
structural, 46–48
and virility, 80
youth on youth, 45, 60

W
War on drugs, 23, 24, 26–29, 44, 47,
91, 93–94

Y
Youth, 16, 33, 43–64, 96–97, 106
as construct, 52, 61
and juvenile justice system, 112
and responsibility, 45–47, 61, 64
transition to adulthood, 60–62,
64

The manufacturer's authorised representative in the EU is Springer
Nature Customer Service Centre GmbH, Europaplatz 3, 69115 Heidelberg,
Germany. If you have any concerns regarding our products, please
contact ProductSafety@springernature.com

Printed and bound by CPI Group (UK) Ltd, Croydon, CR0 4YY
24/04/2026
02096315-0009